SCHOLA

create
and
display

Themes

Full of exciting activities and displays for the whole curriculum

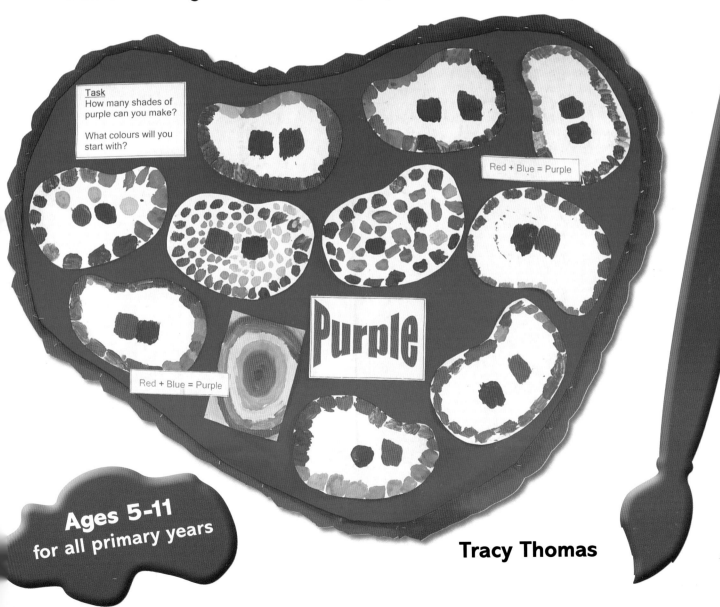

Task
How many shades of
purple can you make?

What colours will you
start with?

Red + Blue = Purple

Red + Blue = Purple

Purple

Ages 5–11
for all primary years

Tracy Thomas

Book End, Range Road, Witney, Oxfordshire, OX29 OYD
www.scholastic.co.uk

© 2011, Scholastic Ltd

1 2 3 4 5 6 7 8 9   0 1 2 3 4 5 6 7 8 9

British Library Cataloguing-in-Publication Data
A catalogue record for this book is available from the
British Library.

ISBN 978-1407-11916-8
Printed by Bell & Bain Ltd, Glasgow

Text © 2011 Tracy Thomas

Commissioning Editor
Paul Naish

Editor
Janice Baiton

Project Editor
Rhiannon Findlay

Series Designer and Cover Design
Andrea Lewis

Photography
Steve Forest

Acknowledgements

Tracy Thomas would like to thank the children of
Claygate Primary School, particularly Oak, Alder,
Elm, Chestnut, Hazel and Sycamore classes (2007–
08) for their amazing enthusiasm, inspiration
and talent in producing the artwork for *Create &
Display: Themes*. The children have risen to the
many different challenges presented in this book
by allowing their imagination and skills to develop,
responding bravely to the creative opportunities. A
big thank you is due to the many staff and parents
for their continued interest, help, encouragement
and support. I had a fantastic year and was part
of a great team. Thank you also to headteacher
Darryl Taylor whose open mindedness to a creative
curriculum supported this exciting project.

Finally, a big thank you to all my family and
friends who have been enthusiastic and excited
about this book, providing practical materials,
encouragement, support and love.

Mixed Sources
Product group from well-managed
forests and other controlled sources
www.fsc.org Cert no. TT-COC-002769
© 1996 Forest Stewardship Council
FSC

Contents

Introduction

- When a cross-curricular approach is used, it is easy to see the learning benefits. The children can see the relevance of the lesson and gain knowledge from different sources. It is a fantastic tool for developing investigation and enquiry skills. A cross-curricular approach allows a theme to develop and to be approached from different angles – for example, the Seaside may lend itself to Literacy, Design and Technology, Drama, Geography and Science – so children can gradually extend their ideas and knowledge. Art is a powerful and exciting way of engaging the children in their learning and can be used to bring all curriculum areas together in a stimulating and creative approach.

- The work in this book was produced by Year 1, 2 and 3 children, but many of the ideas can be adapted and extended for Key Stage 2. The themes can be used as a weekly planning guide for a term's topic, or they can be dipped

into and ideas taken from one chapter and used in another. Many of the activities can be used in different themes – for example, the Pop Art leaves in Mother Nature could be adapted and used in themes such as People and Faces.

- High expectations of every child is an important element of any successful art lesson. Children arrive with different levels of ability, experiences and expectations of their work. All will respond to positive encouragement and interest from the teacher, irrespective of their ability. They may not be the best at drawing, but they can appreciate the colour and texture of their work and see how they have improved. Art develops children's observational skills, encouraging them to enquire and think for themselves by processing information, questioning and evaluating their work. Make sure they have plenty of opportunities to communicate their ideas in a class or a group while working on their shared or individual activities. This will help them enjoy learning and develop their creativity in a secure yet challenging environment.

- Training the children is another important element for success in any art class. It allows the children to be independent learners as they begin to know what resources are available and how to use them. From the start of the year, ensure that the children know where everything is kept and how to use the various resources. This will happen if the children are involved in packing away and organising materials. Spend time in the first term involving the children in the organisation and collection of appropriate materials as this encourages them to take responsibility for their learning and ideas. The children also need to be responsible for their own area and to organise their workspace. This can be achieved even with young children with plenty of support and training at the beginning of the year.

- I hope this book provides many creative and stimulating sessions for you and your class. Enjoy!

Tracy Thomas

Sculpture

Sculpture is a great way to introduce shape, form and texture to the children – it is a real hands-on opportunity to form images from solid materials. The children will have the opportunity to explore ideas about sculpture and learn about the work of sculptors, using a range of materials from natural to man-made. It will encourage the children to look and to make decisions when considering the sensory qualities of materials. Involve the class in collecting the materials they will be using by giving each child a list of materials needed, such as metal, plastic, wood, paper, fabric and natural materials.

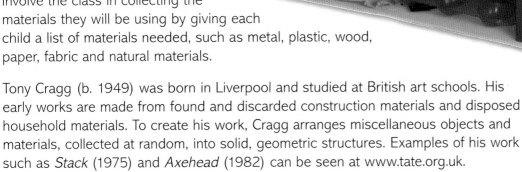

Tony Cragg (b. 1949) was born in Liverpool and studied at British art schools. His early works are made from found and discarded construction materials and disposed household materials. To create his work, Cragg arranges miscellaneous objects and materials, collected at random, into solid, geometric structures. Examples of his work such as *Stack* (1975) and *Axehead* (1982) can be seen at www.tate.org.uk.

Cube in Multimedia

- Ask the children what is sculpture and what does a sculptor do? Check if they know what materials are used to make sculptures. Show a picture of *Stack* by Tony Cragg on the whiteboard. Encourage the children to discuss the materials used and the shapes they see.
- Show the children a variety of sculptures, either pictures or real examples. Challenge their ideas about the materials used and shapes that can make a sculpture.
- Ask the children to collect junk from home. Give them a letter to take home requesting keys, nuts and bolts, plastic bottles, pots, wooden bits and a variety of objects.
- Arrange the various materials on four square pieces of plastic sheeting. Group the materials into metals, plastics and woods and put the different materials on different levels. Use Lego® blocks to support the corners and the centre to allow space between the pieces of plastic sheet.

- Group the children so that they work on different layers of the cube. Encourage them to use plenty of glue to stick on the metal pieces.
- This sculpture could be created as a cylinder or triangular prism – the choice is yours. Plastic bottles between the layers would also be very effective.

Cross-curricular Links

- **Maths** – This work would be a good introduction for 3D shape work. Explore the properties of a cube and other shapes. Start by cutting along the seams of a box of cereal and see what shapes make up a cuboid.
- **ICT** – Program a floor robot, such as a *Pixie*, *Beebot* or *Turtle* to move in a shape.
- **Science** – This activity fits well into a topic on Materials.

Human Figures

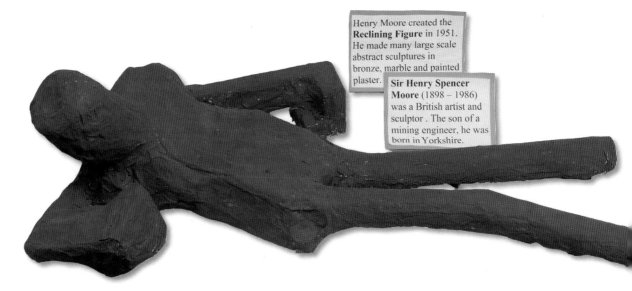

Henry Moore created the **Reclining Figure** in 1951. He made many large scale abstract sculptures in bronze, marble and painted plaster. **Sir Henry Spencer Moore** (1898 – 1986) was a British artist and sculptor. The son of a mining engineer, he was born in Yorkshire.

- Look at *The Reclining Figure* (1951) by Henry Moore (1898–1986). Moore is best known for his large-scale abstract cast bronze and carved marble sculptures. During PE lessons, explore the shapes the body can make by physically trying some positions as a class. Make star shapes and try balancing on two or three body parts. Hold some of the positions and discuss the different joints that will provide a change of direction. Talk about the shapes of the body and limbs.
- If possible, make a large collection of sculptures. Ask the children to bring in smaller examples from home. These commercial varieties are usually made from bronze, marble and plastic. Look closely at the sculptures, noticing the smooth finish and the simple body parts.
- Give the children a piece of clay and ask them to create an image of themselves walking, lying, sitting or moving in some way. Ask them to think about the shape of the arms and the body. The children do not need to worry about details such as fingers or eyes, but encourage them to make the pieces smooth.
- When dry, paint the clay sculptures with silver paint mixed with a little PVA glue. Painting with one solid colour is very effective.

- Following on from the individual clay people, make a large 3D figure from boxes and tubes. Cover the structure in large sheets of newspaper and tape it together.
- Papier mâché the whole statue with strips of torn newspaper and cellulose paste powder. It will need several layers of newspaper to make it thick and strong.
- As the statue will take a few days to dry, aim to leave it for a week before painting with one colour.

Cross-curricular Links

- **Art/Design & Technology** – Look at the work of Barbara Hepworth (1903–75), particularly *Family of Man* (1970) in bronze. She works with materials such as stone and wood. Use her statues as a starting point for the creation of other sculptures showing the human figure.

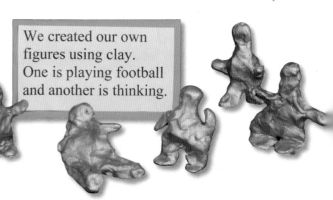

We created our own figures using clay. One is playing football and another is thinking.

Mobiles

- Alexander Calder (1898–1976) was an American sculptor and artist who is famous for inventing the mobile. In 1956 he created a sculpture called *Red Mobile* from painted sheet metal and metal rods. An example of this work can be found at www.calder/org/.
- Ask the class what they know about mobiles and where they have seen a mobile. Look at the pictures of sculptures in *The Surreal Calder* by Mark Rosenthal (Yale University Press, 2005). Discuss the materials Calder used in his mobiles.
- Make a class collection of objects that could be used to make a mobile, such as old keys, metal washers and plastic pots.

- Working in small groups, give each group a coat hanger on which to hang their collection of items. Organise the groups so that one group has plastic bottles, another plastic wheels, another old keys and so on.
- Explain that each group should hang keys, nuts, plastic bottles or paper using sewing thread or string along the hanger. Use different lengths of thread to obtain different levels.
- Ask the children to identify qualities in their sculpture that they like, encouraging them to look at it from all angles.

Paper Sculpture

- Begin by challenging the children's views on sculpture. Ask whether a sculpture can be made from paper and does it have to last forever.
- Give each child two sheets of newspaper. Fold the paper over several times until it becomes two long strips of newspaper. Press down firmly along the edges so it does not unravel.
- Ask the children to join their two pieces of paper together using masking tape. They will then have a small sculpture that they can join with the person next to them. This sculpture can then be joined to other children's sculptures on their table. Gradually the sculpture grows as everyone's work is combined.
- It is helpful to have a frame made from plywood to which parts of the sculpture can be stapled. This gives it height and some stability. As groups finish, staple their pieces to the frame.

Cross-curricular Links

- **Literacy/Design & Technology** – Read *Interpreting Caro* by Paul Moorhouse (Tate Publishing, 2005) to the class. This is a very interesting book that supports modern ways of interpreting sculpture. It introduces the work of Sir Anthony Alfred Caro (b. 1924), an abstract sculptor who abandoned conventional methods of sculpture. Discuss with the children the materials he has used and the shapes he has made. Allow the children to build sculptures with different construction toys such as Polydron, Geomag sticks, etc.
- **Art/Design & Technology** – Barbara Hepworth and Henry Moore use wood, stone and bronzes in their work. Compare their different styles. Then discuss the difference between Anthony Caro and Barbara Hepworth, developing the children's opinions and ideas of art they like.
- **Display** – Put together a class display showing the variety of sculptures made by the children.

Autumn Sculptures

- This activity gives the children great opportunities for collecting a range of autumn objects. Begin by walking around the school pointing out and collecting leaves and seeds. Also encourage the children to bring in leaves from their gardens.
- Cut out large circles, leaf shapes or random shapes on firm card.
- Working in pairs, ask the children to sort a collection of leaves and then collage each shape with one type of leaf or seed. When the circle is covered with seeds or leaves, ask the children to cover it with thin PVA glue using a thick brush to give the work a shiny finish.
- Arrange the shapes on a large board so that they can be bent out to give the sculpture depth.

Forest Sculptures

- To create forest mobiles, make a collection of 'treasures' such as leaves, conkers, winged maple seeds, bark and fir cones. If possible, send a letter home asking for the children to bring in a bag of items to put onto their forest mobile. Ask parents to put holes through conkers and cones to make the activity manageable for the children.
- Begin by threading plenty of tapestry needles with string. Also have scissors and skewers ready to make holes if necessary. Tie a knot at the end of each length of string and use a tapestry needle to thread the 'treasures' onto the string. Start the children off by tying a large fir cone or piece of bark to the end so the string will not come undone.

Autumn Sculpture

Forest Mobiles
We all collected autumn treasures to make these forest mobiles.

Oak and Alder Class worked together to create this Autumn Sculpture.

- When the string is full, the children will need help to tie a loop at the end of the string so the forest mobile can be hung around the school. Alternatively, attach the mobiles to the main display.

Cross-curricular Links

Literacy/ Design & Technology

- Look at *A Collaboration with Nature* by Andy Goldsworthy (Harry N. Abrams, 1990). Goldsworthy uses a range of natural materials for sculpture. Use natural materials from a walk around school such as sticks, stones, and branches to create large sculptures in the playground.
- Read *Midsummer Snowballs* by Andy Goldsworthy (Harry N. Abrams, 2001). This is a fantastic stimulus for discussion with children. Goldsworthy placed large snowballs weighing one ton each around London on Midsummer Night in 2000. The responses of the public are recorded and photographed. The book introduces a great debate around the topic of sculpture.

Exploring Nature

This is a great theme at any time of the year but especially in autumn when change is happening so fast that children can easily observe it. The following activities explore line, shape, colour and texture in their natural forms. The children have the opportunity to touch and gain a feeling about nature from first-hand experience. Encourage them to observe closely what they are collecting. Use their collections for collage work and close observation.

Mother Nature Collage

- Begin by walking around the school to identify plants and collect fallen leaves, bark and any interesting items that the children find. These might include red leaves, hydrangeas, bamboo, sycamore keys, grasses, bark, sticks, heather, rose hips, oak leaves – the list is extensive. If possible, write to parents to involve them in helping the children collect items to use in this activity.
- Working in pairs, make a collage from a piece of square card covered in one of the natural objects collected. For a larger collage, the children could make two squares covered with the same objects.
- The children will need to use a sufficient amount of glue so that materials such as conkers and sticks adhere firmly to the card. Allow plenty of time for the glue to dry properly.
- To display, place the squares in a three by nine arrangement (or smaller or larger as applicable) with a bright border so it looks like one picture.

Pop Art Leaves

- Using a collection of leaves, discuss with the children their shape and pattern. Provide some laminated leaves for the children to examine in detail.
- Draw a leaf onto thin card and cut out a shape that resembles the leaves collected. Stick the leaf shape onto a square piece of thick cardboard and add the veins and a little detail. You now have a printing block of a leaf shape. Allow to dry before using.
- Roll a printing roller in a tray of paint and cover the block with paint by rolling over the leaf. When the block is covered, turn it over and print onto cartridge paper. Repeat using another colour and print. Arrange leaves next to each other using two or three different colour paints.
- This technique will give the effect of Pop Art made famous by the American artist Andy Warhol (1928–87), who used images from mass–produced culture and repeated the same image with different colours. Use *Art Revolutions Pop Art* by Linda Bolton (Belitha Press, 2000) as a stimulus.
- Display the pictures with the printing blocks to demonstrate how the process was achieved.

Symmetrical Leaves

- Provide some laminated leaves for the children to examine closely. Use magnifying glasses to develop the children's observation skills. Point out that the edge of a leaf is rarely straight and tends to be a little jagged.

- Supply the children with a square piece of paper and ask them to fold it into quarters. Ask them choose an interesting-shaped leaf and draw it in pastel in one of the quarters.
- Next the children move to another quarter and

draw the reflection in that square, matching the original leaf. They complete the remaining squares by drawing a reflection in each and so develop an interesting symmetrical pattern.

Cross-curricular Links

- **Science** – Investigate plants in the local environment. Encourage the children to learn the names of some of the plants and trees around the school. Identify them by the leaves and seeds. Look for similarities and differences between the plants. Consider the different habitats that plants grow in.

Nature Fabric Hanging

- Discuss with the children all the wonderful items they have collected during this theme. Talk about what they would like to sew on their wall hanging – leaves, conkers and seeds will make a great display. Hessian is an easy material for children to sew on and tapestry needles that are not sharp can be used to sew pre-cut leaves and thick wool straight onto the hessian to look like stems.

- Provide a collection of materials in rich autumn colours. Encourage the children to bring in different types of materials, such as velvet, from home. Pre-cut some leaves in interesting materials using a range of colours and textures.

- Begin by looking at the different materials, wools and cottons you are going to use. Demonstrate simple fabric joining techniques (for example, sewing, gluing and weaving) as well as some basic stitching (for example, starting, running stitch and ending). Sew with double thread knotted at the bottom so that the thread does not keep pulling off the needle.

- Ask the children to sew the ribbon, thick thread and wool directly onto the hessian. Use large-eyed tapestry needles for this as they are easier to thread with thick wool and ribbon.

- Once they have sewn on most of the fabrics, the children will be able to embellish the wall hanging using beads, threads and other materials that can be stuck on if necessary.

- Encourage the children to think about the textures, colours and shapes on their collage so that they use a variety materials.

- Display hangings individually or sewn onto a large piece of material with a bamboo stick at the top and bottom. Tie some ribbon onto the ends of the top bamboo stick to create a wall hanging.

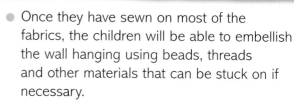

Georgia O'Keeffe

Georgia O'Keeffe (1887–1986) was one of the most influential painters in twentieth century American art. She is most famous for her close-up paintings of flowers. During her thirties she started painting flowers in a way no one else had ever done before. She focused on a part of a flower head and magnified it so that it filled an entire canvas.

Georgia O'Keeffe focused on part of a flower head and magnified it so that it filled an entire canvas.

By transforming them from small, fragile objects into large ones, she was expressing her love of nature.

The edges of the petals were often cut off. She painted flowers so large that they seem as close up to the viewer as the flowers themselves might seem to a passing butterfly.

Colour Mix Flowers

- Look at O'Keeffe's work and notice how she blends one colour into the next, making sure the brushstrokes are invisible. *Red Canna* (1923) and *Red Poppy* (1927) are good examples of her magnified work. O'Keeffe wrote about her flower paintings,
  "I have painted what each flower is to me and I have painted it big enough so that others would see what I see."
- Provide a bunch of chrysanthemums, or any brightly coloured flowers where the structure of the flowers is simple so that the children's painting will not be complicated by too many layers.
- Give the children magnifying glasses to get really close and observe the detail. Also allow the children to hold the flowers. Discuss which part or segment of the flower

they would like to paint: the whole, a half or a quarter.
- On square piece of cartridge paper, encourage the children to make their strokes large. They will need to use all the paper.
- Provide mixing trays and an appropriate selection of paints so the children can mix the colours gradually and build up a range of colours.
- Encourage the children to mix a slightly different shade of purple by adding more blue and to overlap a few petals because petals do not all sit next to each in a uniform manner.

Cross-curricular Links

- **Art** – This activity could be done with pastels. Encourage the children to blend the different colours on the page. Alternatively they could use torn pieces of tissue paper layered to achieve the blend and depth of colour.
- **Science** – Cut a straight line through a flower and make a drawing of the different parts of the flower. Label the stamen, petals etc. This encourages the children's observational skills.

Investigating Pattern

Pattern is an integral part of our lives, whether in the form of naturally occurring shapes or man-made designs. A pattern is a shape or design that is repeated. This theme gives the children the opportunity to explore how shape and colour can be organised and combined to create patterns. They can experiment with stencilling and a variety of print-making techniques to develop their printing skills.

Pattern Collage

- Ask the children what is a pattern and where have they seen it. Encourage them to collect examples of patterns at home and in the environment. Look closely at how the patterns are made – for example, overlapped or repeated.

- Look at examples of patterns. *Patterns* by Drusilla Cole (Laurence King Publishing, 2007) is a great stimulus for demonstrating the range of possible patterns. Provide some photos showing patterns in temples in Thailand, flooring in Dubai and printed textiles from India to compare designs from different cultures.

- Begin by making the printing tools. Talk about what shapes the children would like to work with and then ask them to cut a shape out of sponge with scissors and stick it onto firm card.

- Encourage the children to experiment with their sponge-printing tool on plain paper and to think about using repeating patterns. Discuss any problems with their printing tool. For example, if they did not cut the sides of their shape away deeply enough, the sides that should not show may print as well.

- Divide a large piece of plain white material into squares and give one to each child.

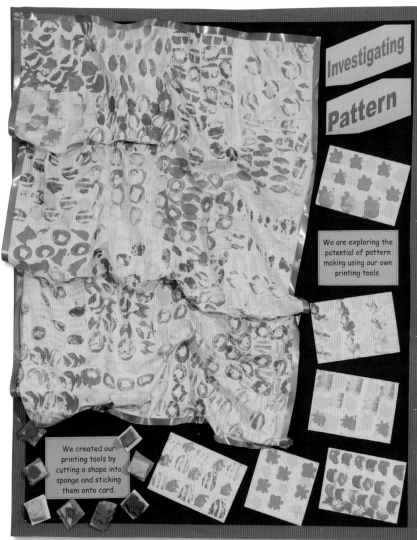

We are exploring the potential of pattern making using our own printing tools.

We created our printing tools by cutting a shape into sponge and sticking them onto card.

- Ask the children to work on their own square using two printing blocks and two colours. They can copy the design they created on paper when experimenting with their sponges or try out a new idea. Encourage them to make a repeating pattern with their colours or shapes.

Stencils

- Begin by exploring the difference between stencil printing and block printing. Demonstrate the two types of printing techniques so that the children can start forming ideas for their design.
- Draw a shape onto a card as a guide to cut around. Show the children how to cut out the shape from a piece of card to make a stencil. Bend the card slightly and make a little hole with scissors, then open up the card and push the scissors through the hole and start cutting along the drawn lines. The children may require help to start cutting out their shape because they need to begin in the middle of the card.
- Make two stencil shapes.
- Begin with one stencil. Use a sponge to print through the stencil shape. Repeat with the same shape but rotate the stencil a quarter turn or a half turn. Continue until the shape is in its original position. Demonstrate rotation, quarter and half turns so the children can gradually see a pattern developing.
- Continue on the next line until the paper is full.
- Take the second stencil and decide whether to overlap or set it in its own space. Begin a repeating pattern with this shape using a contrasting colour.

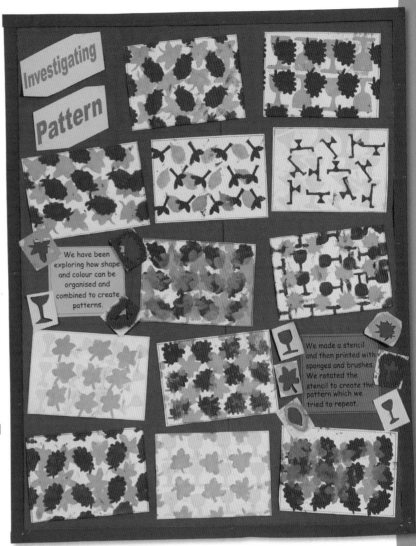

- Consider how a pattern is made – for example, overlapped, repeated, rotated or reflected. Review the patterns the children make and discuss the ways in which they developed their own ideas.

Cross-curricular Links

- **Maths** – Use mathematical vocabulary to describe position, direction and movement. Recognise rotation, reflection and symmetry.
- **ICT** – Ask children to use ICT programs such as *Colour Magic* or *Publisher* to explore:
  - how shape can be copied, re-sized and multiple copies made.
  - how paint software can be used to explore symmetry.
  - how to flood fill shapes with different colours.
  - how to print out a range of repeat patterns.
  - creating a pattern with rotation and a repeating pattern.

Printing with Boards

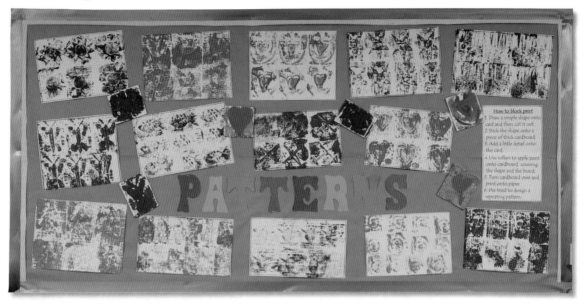

- Read *How Artists Use Pattern and Texture* by Paul Flux (Heinemann, 2001). This book demonstrates how easy it is to create a pattern because a pattern develops when a shape or design is repeated. Discuss with the children where they have seen patterns, such as in nature, on buildings, on materials and on their clothes. This discussion will extend their knowledge and develop their ideas.
- As the children now have some idea about printing, ask them to decide on a design for their printing board. Explore a range of different ideas from flowers, shapes and cars to lines, faces and leaves.

- Give each child a square piece of thick cardboard. Ask the children to draw the shape they have chosen and then cut out and stick it onto the thick cardboard. Allow the glue to dry.
- Use a printing roller to cover the printing block with paint. Dip the roller in the paint, then cover the printing block with a thin layer of paint.
- Turn the piece of card over and print onto some paper. Press firmly and keep the printing block still. Repeat, adding another colour to the printing board and place next to the previous print. Continue until the paper is covered.

Snowflakes Collage

- Encourage the children to bring in green/blue or purple/pink wrapping paper to use in a collage. Make a collection with similar colours of tissue, crepe and shiny paper.
- Ask the children to decide which colours to focus on, encouraging them to use different textures if possible.
- Create a collage of colours by tearing the paper and overlapping the colours to completely cover an A4 piece of sugar paper.
- Cut out a snowflake pattern on white paper by folding a piece

of A4 paper into quarters and cutting out some shapes that will repeat over the paper. Cover the collage with the white paper and the pattern will show through the gaps.

Black and White Patterns

- Look at work of Bridget Riley (b.1931), a wellknown British artist. She is acclaimed as one of the finest exponents of Op-Art, with her subtle variations in size, shape and position of blocks within an overall pattern. Draw attention particularly to *Descending* (1965) and *Movement in Squares* (1961) where she exploits the fallibility of the human eye.
- Victor Vasarely (1906–97) was a Hungarian-born French artist who is often regarded as the father of Op-Art. Working as a graphic artist in the 1930s, he created what is considered the first Op-Art piece – *Zebra* (1938). Concentrate on Vasarely's work *Riu-Kiu-C* (1960). This is a simple picture with straight lines and shapes that the children can easily recognise. An example can be found at www.vasarely.com.
- Explain to the children that they are going to make a black and white picture using strips of black and white card.
- Give each child a 25 cm square of black or white card and some pre-cut strips of black and white card in different thicknesses and lengths.
- Children with a white square will use black strips and those with a black square will use white strips. Provide some scissors and glue.
- Ask the children to arrange the strips of card on their square. They should cut the straight strips to get different lengths and change direction.
- Display by putting all the squares together to create a large square that will give an optical effect.

Wax Resist and Food Colouring

- Show the children some examples of batik printing. Discuss the patterns they can see. Are they repeating?
- Ask the children to design a repeating pattern on a sheet of white A4 paper using white wax crayon. When they are finished, give them several colours of watered-down food colouring to paint onto the paper with a thick

paintbrush. The pattern they have made will show through the food colouring.

- Ask the children to transfer their pattern with any improvements onto a piece of white fabric using white wax crayons.
- Again use a brush to paint the food colouring onto fabric. The colours will merge and the pattern will show through.

Colour

Colour is a vital part of our everyday lives. Artists use colour to express their feelings, create moods and make viewers react in a certain way to their paintings. Colour comes from the light rays that reflect off an object. Artists often explore how this works in their paintings by mixing colours and developing an understanding of which colours go together to achieve the effect they want.

Introducing Colour Mixing

- Colour mixing can be introduced as an investigation for the children to work out. Try to make it exciting. Who can make the most shades? How many shades of purple do you think there are? How can you make the shade darker? These questions are a useful introduction and encourage children to think about what they are going to do while you demonstrate mixing colours. It is important to demonstrate how to mix paints and to gradually change the colour.

- Begin with a paint palette of two small amounts of red and yellow paint and a paintbrush. Dip the paintbrush into the red and move a small amount into a clean space. Next dip the brush into the yellow and add it to the red. Mix together to create a shade of orange, then add a little more yellow. What has happened? Keep adding yellow and let the children observe the gradual change.
- Finish by asking the children to experiment with their own mixing.

Shade Mixing

- In pairs, give the children small amounts of red and blue paint to mix in a paint palette.
- Encourage them to mix and change the colour very slowly.
- Ask the children to paint their two original red and blue colours in the middle of a piece of paper cut in the shape of an artist palette. As the children make the shades of purple, they should paint a blob of each shade around the edge of the palette.
- After a while, give them a little white to add to their mixing experience.
- Display the finished items on backing paper cut in the shape of a palette. Place table in front of the display showing items demonstrating how the children worked, so they can explore further.
- In addition, provide a large piece of plain white sheeting. In turns, give each child a pipette to

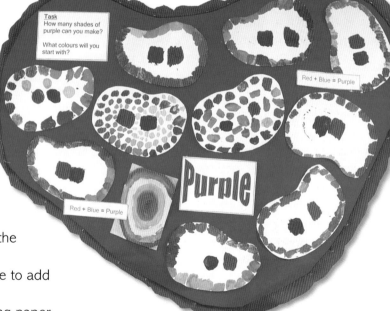

squirt red and blue food colouring on to the sheet, eventually covering the whole area. The colours will gradually carry on mixing after the sheet is full of food colouring. When dry, it will demonstrate how the colours mixed and will provide a red, blue and purple sheet. Use the sheet to display in front of the colour mixing exhibit.

Complementary Colours

- Red, yellow and blue are called primary colours – they cannot be made by mixing together other colours. Secondary colours are made by mixing two primary colours together. Adding more of one colour creates different shades.
- Demonstrate some of these facts on the board using a colour wheel as a useful visual tool. Gradually draw the colour wheel as the children respond to your questions – for example, what colour will I get if I mix yellow and blue?
- Colours on the opposite sides of the wheel complement one another – for example, green and red, yellow and purple, blue and orange. This means that they work together so that they both stand out.

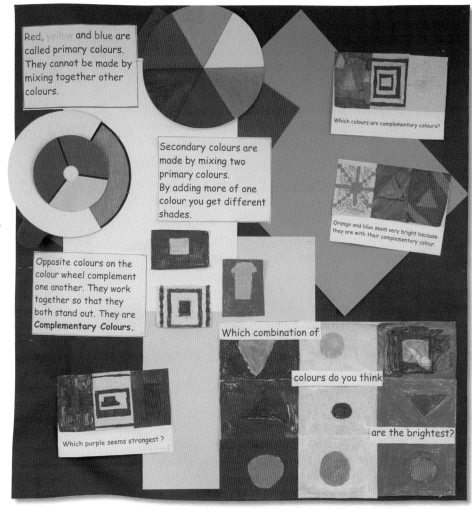

Red, yellow and blue are called primary colours. They cannot be made by mixing together other colours.

Secondary colours are made by mixing two primary colours. By adding more of one colour you get different shades.

Opposite colours on the colour wheel complement one another. They work together so that they both stand out. They are **Complementary Colours**.

Which colours are complementary colours?

Orange and blue seem very bright because they are with their complementary colour.

Which combination of colours do you think are the brightest?

Which purple seems strongest ?

- To test this theory, in groups, ask the children to colour in squared paper with two different combinations of colours to see which combinations stand out the most. This can be done using felt tips, pastels or coloured pencils.
- You will need nine different groups to test the different combinations: 1) blue with green, orange and purple; 2) red with green, orange and purple; 3) yellow with green, orange and purple.
- Display the results on the board and discuss which colour combinations complement each other by making one another stand out.

Cross-curricular Links

- **Science** – Look at the theme Light and Dark as this links well with this colour theme. Objects do not have their own colour. Colour comes from light and it is what we see when light rays are reflected off an object. A beam of light is made up of red, orange, yellow, green, blue, indigo and violet. This range of colours is called the colour spectrum.
  - To observe that light is made up of the colours of the rainbow, you will need a prism and a bright torch. Shine a bright light source through the prism to see the individual colours. On a sunny day you can make a rainbow by spraying water in the playground.
  - The absence of light means the absence of colour. You cannot see colours in the dark, use a black box to test this out. Put some coloured object in the black box to test whether you can see the colours.

Mood Boards

- Look at *Apples and Oranges* (c.1899) by Paul Cezanne (1839–1906) and discuss how he used warm colours to give this picture strength. The warm colours bring the scene to life, making ordinary objects seem extra special.
- Red, yellow and orange are warm colours and artists often use these colours to show strong feelings such as happiness and excitement. Blue, green and grey are cool colours, which make us think of the sky and sea. When artists use cool colours, their pictures can seem cold or calm, thoughtful or sad.
- In groups, give the children a large letter to collage with the appropriate colours. Give the children with W, A, R and M the warm tissue colours to collage their letters, and the children with C, O, L and D the cold tissue colours of different shades of blue and green.

- Display with the word COLOURS running down the middle and COLD and WARM arranged on either side.

Colour Filters

- Look closely at some large flowers with the children. Encourage them to notice the petal shapes and parts of the flower such as the stamen. Artificial lilies arranged on the tables are useful resources that the children can examine closely.
- Give the children a coloured filter – a piece of thin transparent plastic – through which they can look at the lilies. Coloured cellophane serves the same purpose. Blue, green and red filters work well.
- On pieces of white cartridge paper, ask the children to use pastels to draw the lily in the colours they see through the filter. If blue, the stem and leaves should be dark blue while the petals are a pale blue.
- Encourage the children to mix colours of varying shades of lightness and darkness. They will also need to use a little green to give the leaves a blue-green tinge. They should blend the pastels with small pieces of kitchen roll or their fingers. By standing over their drawing, they can drag the piece of kitchen roll up the stem blending the colours as they travel along it.
- The drawings will show a variety of shades of the filters' original colour. The effect of the different filters give the drawings very different feels – some are warm while others are cool and clean.

Try looking through the colour filters and then use the pastels to blend the colour you can see.

Shades of Colour

We mixed, yellow, white, orange and ███ paint to make these different shades of colour.

- Paul Klee (1879–1940) was born in Switzerland to a musical family. He turned to painting in his teenage years and became fascinated by colour. He said, 'Colour has taken possession of me.' He taught colour mixing and colour theory to his university students.
- Look at Paul Klee's work *Rose Garden* (1920) and *Rhythmical, Stricter and Freer* (1930) with the children and discuss the colours and shapes used to make the paintings.
- Demonstrate mixing the paints. The children can be very responsive when you mix in front of them. Encourage them to predict changes when adding different colours.
- Give the children red, yellow and white with which to work.
- Using square pieces of paper, ask the children to mix their colours and paint a square. By constantly adding different combinations, they should build up a wide range of shades of colours.
- Display the finished pieces in two squares of four by four or three by three. The effect is very dramatic.

Cross-curricular Links

- **Literacy** – *Hailstones and Halibut Bones* by Mary O'Neill (Doubleday Books, 1989) has many poems about colour. This makes an interesting starting point for the children to write poems about their feelings and what colours mean to them.
- **Art/Literacy** – Look at different paintings and encourage the children to discuss and write about the colours in the pictures and how they make them feel. Two great paintings to stimulate discussion are:
  – *Portrait of the Artist's Mother* (1871) by James Whistler (1834–1903). He painted this picture in cold, dark colours such as black, white and green-grey. How does he want us to see his mother? What sort of mood is he trying to create?
  – *California Seascape* (1968) by David Hockney (b.1937). This picture uses mainly cool colours but the artist includes a few warmer colours that make a lot of difference, lifting the painting and giving it some warmth.

Shape

Our world is full of shapes – they are everywhere. Some artists arrange shapes so we can recognise objects such as a square, others use shapes that are abstract and have no name. Artists can use shapes to make us look at a picture in a particular way. Shapes are often used to give a message that is clear – for example, an arrow – and sometimes the shapes are open to interpretation. Shapes can be two dimensional with width and height, or three dimensional with height, width and depth.

2D Circles

- Wassily Kandinsky (1866–1944) was a Russian painter. He is credited with painting the first modern abstract works.
- Look at Wassily Kandinsky's *Squares with Concentric Circles* (1913). This painting provides an interesting starting point for looking at shapes. Encourage the children to think about the shapes he used, as well as increasing and decreasing shapes and sizes.
- Explain to the children that they will be cutting out circles of different sizes and arranging them accordingly.
- This activity is good for all levels of ability as it develops the children's fine motor skills.

- Provide the children with scissors, glue, sugar paper and card in different sizes and colours.
- Ask the children to start by cutting out some 25 cm circles in card. Next they need to cut out six to ten circles with each one being gradually smaller in size.
- Encourage the children to cut all their circles and arrange them before they glue them together. This will allow them to see how the circles look and decide whether they would like to add another in the middle, for instance between the third and fourth circle.
- Arrange the circles on a board (ideally circular) and hang some in front of the display.

3D Shape Collage

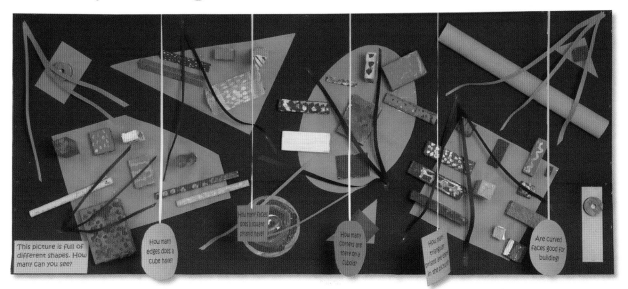

- Look at further work by Wassily Kandinsky such as *Swinging* (1925) and *Compositions* (1923). Talk about the paintings and encourage the children to tell you what they see.
- Encourage the children to collect a variety of 3D shapes such as cuboids, pyramids, cubes, triangular prisms, cylinders and spheres. A range of sizes from very small to large can be useful.
- Ask the children to paint the shapes in a variety of colours and decorate them.
- When dry, the children can arrange the shapes on pre-cut card of various shapes. Provide four or five large pieces of card in the shape of a circle, a square, a triangle and a pentagon. Try to place some of the cuboids and flat-sided shapes on their ends so they stand tall. These look great on the wall as they give the picture depth.
- When dry, arrange the four or five shapes on a black background. Cut a few strips of coloured card to display 'jumping' over the shapes to add a 3D effect.
- Hang some questions about the picture and about shapes in general in front of the display. This will encourage the children to look closely at the display.

Cross-curricular Links

- **Design & Technology** – Make cubes and cuboids from paper straws and pipe cleaners. This will reinforce the children's knowledge of the number of corners, faces and edges a shape has. These can hang as part of the display.
  – Make 3D shapes from templates, again reinforcing knowledge of shapes. Present as an activity to do in front of the display.
  – Cut open boxes (cuboids or cubes) and stick different coloured paper on the faces of the cuboids. Display these on the sides of a large painted cuboid. This is a great visual learning tool. Add some questions about cuboids to extend the children's learning and to develop their observational skills.
  – Paint large shapes, such as cylinders, with questions – for example, how many faces does a cylinder have?
- **Maths** – Create some investigations that can be laminated and displayed in front of the picture with whiteboard markers to encourage the children to interact with the display. For example, one side of a square cube is 5 centimetres. How many centimetres is it all the way around the square cube?

Square and Rectangular Painting

silver   texture   dark blue   shades   structure

white   mixing   blend   turquoise   bright blue

- Look at the work of artist Jo Last (b. 1962). Examples can be found on her website at www.joannelast.co.uk. Her abstract work uses shades of colour with overlapping squares and rectangles.
- Discuss the pictures, looking at the shades used and how overlapping the shapes gives a picture some depth, as if some of the shapes are on top of the others.
- Demonstrate how to mix paints in a paint palette. Give the children shades of a colour in wells and also white and silver for mixing. Encourage the children to mix in one well and to keep changing the shade by adding a little paint from the selection.
- Invite the children to share a palette in pairs – this encourages conversation and investigation. Encourage them to take turns and discuss the colours they are trying to make. While sharing a palette they should each have their own piece of A3 cartridge paper on which to work.
- While looking at Jo Last's paintings, observe the texture of some of the rectangles and discuss how this can be achieved.
- After the children have put some colour on their paper, encourage them to: swirl their brush around in a circular motion – holding

in one place each time makes circles on their work; use a thinner brush to add thicker colour to the space; use utensils to drag across their work to make lines or patterns.
- Encourage the children to use a little silver at the end of their painting as this will stand out and give the work a strong finish.

Malevich Shape

- Kazimir Malevich (1878–1935) was a Russian painter and a pioneer of geometric abstract art. This type of art was based on the use of simple shapes being placed in a space in their own right. Malevich was the founder of Suprematism, a Russian abstract art movement which banished every trace of subject and relies solely on the interaction between form and colour.
- In *Suprematist Composition* (1915), Malevich uses red, orange and black overlapping, geometric shapes to evoke a sense of depth.
- In *Suprematism* (1915), geometric shapes are painted in base colours and appear to float as if suspended on the canvas.

- Show the children the two paintings by Malevich and discuss how he has made the painting look three dimensional. This can be shown by placing some pre-cut pieces of a card next to each other on a whiteboard. The effect will be that the shapes look very flat. By moving a few over each other and overlapping them, the picture suddenly has depth.
- Provide the children with some different sized colourful rectangular pieces of card on which to work. Also provide some shapes for the children to draw around, a selection of card for cutting up as well as rulers, pencils and glue.
- Encourage the children to cut all their shapes out and to arrange them on the card before they start to glue.

Toys

Toys are more that just playthings for children, they are a very important part of a child's life. They can extend a child's imagination and develop their learning experience. They help children deal with issues such as possession and sharing as they grow up. It is a theme that children instantly relate to and because it interests them greatly, it can be used to hold their attention in order to teach educational concepts.

The Teddy Robber

- Read the story *The Teddy Robber* by Ian Beck (Picture Corgi, 2006). It is a story of a giant who takes children's teddy bears in the middle of the night because he has lost his favourite teddy. The story provides great opportunities for discussions about the giant's behaviour. Was he justified to take others' teddies? How else could he have dealt with his problem of the lost teddy?
- The part of the story depicting the cupboard containing all the teddies that the giant has taken is good for reproducing visually. Provide the children with many different styles of teddy shapes between 15 and 25 cm tall. The teddies will need to be displayed on their sides, sitting, standing and lying down because they are just dumped in the cupboard when the giant realises they are not the teddy he is looking for.
- Invite the children to make several different types of teddy using a variety of materials. For example:
  - Cut up pieces of fur for the children to stick onto their teddy.
  - Cut up balls of wool for children to stick onto teddies to make interesting hairy teddies.
  - Use brown and gold crepe paper to create teddies with a fringed effect.
  - Create pastel drawings of the teddies that the children have provided.
  - Use thick material in creams and browns cut up and ready to stick on.
- Use some bright brown paper as a background for a display and cut up gold wrapping paper as shelves for the teddies to sit on.
  - Add a few small real teddies to give the picture depth.
  - When the display is completed, read the book again and ask the children to draw and write about their favourite part of the story.

Stuffed Teddy Bears

- Encourage the children to supply their own teddies.
- Discuss why these are special, how old the teddies are and their names.
- Introduce the idea that the children are going to make their own teddies by sewing pieces of material together.
- Pre-cut different coloured teddies in felt as this is colourful and soft and easier for young children to work with.
- Demonstrate how to sew around the edge of a teddy. Start just below the head and sew around the edge to the other side of the head. Now stuff the teddy with a soft filling. When the teddy has stuffing in his legs, arms and body, finish sewing around the edge of his head.

- Decorate the teddies with fur for their tummies, buttons for their eyes and various other pieces of material for clothes.
- Encourage the children to give the teddies a name and the decorating can suit the different characters.
- Add some of the finished teddies to the class display and present others on their own.

Cross-curricular Links

- **Art** – Create some pastel observational drawings of the children's favourite toys.
- **History** – Visit a toy museum or invite a toy museum to visit your school. They can bring old and new toys to compare and discuss.
  – Encourage the children to bring in old and new toys. Look at the similarities and differences between toys today and in the past. How have the toys changed and what were the toys made from? What were toys like when the children's parents or grandparents were young? Encourage the children to think about the changes in their own lives and in those of their family or adults around them. This provides excellent opportunities for children to develop their speaking and listening skills.
  – Draw a timeline of children's toys from a Chinese kite in 800 BCE, to tin plate toys in 1910 to hand-held computer games in 2000.
- **Drama** – In *The Teddy Robber* explore how Tom felt when he thought he was going to lose his teddy. In pairs the children can act out the conversation between Tom and the giant after he had locked all the teddies away.

Baboushka

- *Baboushka* is a Russian folk tale retold by Arthur Scholey (Lion Hudson, 2002). It tells the story of a lady who is visited by the Three Kings on their way to see the new-born baby Jesus. They invite her to travel with them but she leaves late and misses seeing the baby. The story says she is still looking for the baby Jesus and leaves a toy for young children as she continues her journey.
- Read the story to the children and compare it to the traditional Christmas nativity story. Talk about the lady's loneliness and why she is still looking for the baby Jesus. Ask the children to choose their favourite part of the story to use for a pop-up book.
- To make a pop-up book, fold an A4 piece of card in half either way. Ask the children to draw a background on the back piece of card and encourage them to fill it in with details from the story – maybe the house and trees around it. Create a pop-up strip by making two vertical cuts down the fold of the card and pulling the strip of card forward. Ask the children to draw Baboushka and a king and stick them on the pop-up strip so they stand up. When finished, ask the children to write the story on the lower piece of card. A simple sentence is fine for five year olds, while a little more is possible for older children.
- Pop-up books look good on a large display of the story.

- For the background, print on A3 white paper with blue marbling ink.
- Use yellow sugar paper printed with gold, yellow and beige paint for a sandy road at the bottom of the picture.
- Cut out different shapes of houses and paint with a variety of golden, yellow and brown colours and add windows using gold paint. Mix some sand and glue into the paint to give it a thick gritty texture for rough houses.
- Make one large tree with rolled up pieces of green tissue and crepe. Create the trunk with shades of brown paint on brown paper.
- Make numerous small Christmas trees to place among the houses to give the picture depth. Cut out pieces of green cellophane, tissue, crepe and shiny paper, adding small cuts to the edges. Start by sticking these at the bottom of the trees then overlapping the pieces of paper.
- Baboushka can be made from materials stapled onto the picture. Use an old piece of material for her skirt and ruffle it so that it looks full and her body does not appear flat. Do the same for her blouse and head scarf. Staple the material around the handle of a basket so this can support a few toys.
- Make some stars from paper straws and pipe cleaners. Show the children how to make two triangles from the straws and stick the triangles on top of each other to make a star shape. Add a little glitter.

Hinged Father Christmas

- Pre-cut all the parts of the Santa's body. For each Santa you will need:
  - two triangles for the body and hat, and four rectangles for legs and arms in red card;
  - one triangle for a beard, a rectangle for the belt and a small circle for the pom-pom on the hat in white;
  - a circle for the face;
  - two black circles for feet and two glove-shaped pieces.
- Ask the children to join the parts by making holes in the card and securing together using split pins. They may need a little help making the small holes to push the split pins through the card.

- Attach the legs and arms to the body. The head and the beard can be attached to the body at the same time.
- Attach the hat with the pompom to the head.
- Join the feet and hands to the legs and arms.
- The Santa will be able to move at all the places joined by the split pins.
- When finished, ask the children to draw on a face.

Investigating Materials

The children should be given the opportunity to handle and discuss various materials in groups and as a class. This will allow them to gain sensory experience of materials and an understanding of colour and texture. Materials are the substances of which things are made. Encourage the chldren to communicate their ideas about the best materials for different purposes to help gain a clearer understanding of the properties of materials around them.

Materials Collage

- Before attempting this activity, collect a wide variety of materials. Make collections of wood, plastic, fabric, glass, metal, clay and paper. Two useful series of books are *I Know That!* (by Claire Llewellyn; Franklin Watts, 2004) and *Materials* (by Chris Oxlade; Heinemann, 2001).
- Before the lesson, cut out a large shape to fit the area you have for display – you will need to stick several pieces of card together. The larger the shape, the better the impact.
- Begin the lesson by reading one of the books from the *Materials* series such as *Wood* and discuss the questions raised in the book. Does wood float? Is it rough or smooth? If there is time at the end of the session, read a different book from the

series and compare the two materials.
- In groups or pairs, ask the children to stick the different materials – two children could stick wood, while another two stick marbles, and another two stick plastic lids or nuts and bolts. Gradually fill up all the space. All the children should have worked on a different part of the collage.
- Allow plenty of time for materials to dry as a lot of PVA glue is needed for sticking metal and heavier objects.
- Ask a colleague to help to put the collage on the wall because it will be heavy.

Paper Collage

- For this activity, you will need a collection of brown paper picture frames such as the ones used for school photos. A variety of sizes is useful so that the display is varied.
- The aim of the activity is to investigate different types of paper and to explore the effects of folding, scrunching, tearing, cutting, pleating, rolling, twisting, curling and stretching.
- Provide a collection of different types of paper on a tray and tell the children they are going to find out all the different things they can do with paper. Ask them for ideas and demonstrate each suggestion.
- Give the children a variety of paper – tissue, crepe, sugar, shiny, thin and thick paper. It is effective to use a group of colours together – for example, red, yellow and orange make an interesting contrast.
- Provide each child with a photo frame in which to display their work.

Individual Collages

- Begin by reading a book from the *Materials* series, such as *Metal*. Encourage the children to think of words to describe metal.
- Provide small pieces of card and PVA glue for the children to design their own collages. They can make a collage using just one material or a selection of materials.

Willow Fabric Weaving

Look carefully at the different fabrics through a magnifying glass. Explore the construction of the fabrics. How do you think the fabrics are made?

We attempted to collage the bamboo structures using simple weaving techniques. We used many different types of fabric. Which woven bamboo do you like the look and feel of best?

We have been exploring the different textures and surfaces of various fabrics that we collected. Some are smooth while others are rough. They all have a different feel about them.

Bamboo Weaving

- Discuss the word 'fabric' and the variety of items made from fabric.
- Make a collection of fabrics that the children like. How do the fabrics make them feel? Describe the texture of different fabrics. Group them in different ways, such as how they feel or by thickness.
- Look closely at the fabrics with magnifying glasses and explore their construction. How do the children think the fabrics are made?
- Discuss looms and basic weaving techniques. Demonstrate simple weaving using strips of paper and explore different patterns, such as over/under, over two and under one.

- In groups, invite the children to work on a loom. Use a latticed bamboo frame for weaving with different textures and colours of material. The children can tie the material to one end of the frame, weave to the other end and then tie the material to that end of the frame. If some pieces of material do not go completely across the frame, these can be tied in the middle.
- If you have a beam, display the frames hanging from the ceiling. Alternatively, fix frames to a display board by stapling the materials just under the bamboo junctions.

Plastic Bag Weaving

- Sharon Porteous (b. 1971) has developed a technique of making textiles through recycling mainly plastic carrier bags. She produces functional objects such as *Pull Cord Carrier* (1998) and decorative objects such as the *Elongated Woven Hanging* (2001).
- Provide a large loom made from wood at least 60 cm by 90 cm. Use a staple gun to fix some string or plastic strips along the frame with wide slots. This is the warp and it needs to be taut so the plastic bag strips can weave between it.
- Collect many different colours of plastic bags and cut them into strips.

- Tie the plastic strips to one side of the frame on the wood and weave them in and out of the warp. Take the plastic bag strips across to the other side of the loom and tie them on the wood. If the strips do not go completely across, tie them to the warp and then start with another colour.

Sharon Porteous has developed a technique of making textiles by recycling plastic bags.

How many different coloured plastic bags can you see in the weaving?

Plastic Bag Weaving

Planet Collages

- Ask the children to draw a picture using their knowledge of planets and the solar system – their inspiration can come from memory and their imagination.
- Provide a piece of black material, felt, buttons and a collection of 'jewels' that have a hole so the children can attach them to the material. Use a piece of card to mount the material on when finished, to give the collage a firm base.
- Invite the children to cut out planets in a

Cross-curricular Links

- **Science** – Materials have many properties that can be recognised using our senses. Get the children to handle a variety of objects and introduce language such as shiny, dull, hard, soft, bendy, spiky, smooth and rough. The objects can be scientifically sorted according to their properties.
  – When considering the properties of materials, encourage the children to

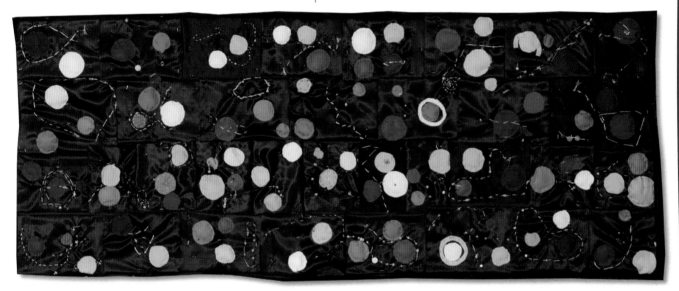

variety of colours. Demonstrate how to attach the felt planets by sewing, showing the beginning, middle and finishing off.
- After sewing halfway around the planet, give the children a little stuffing that can be sewn into the planet. This gives the work a 3D look. Ask the children to create at least three planets before starting on the detail.
- Use gold and silver thread to sew directly onto the material as a ring around a planet or as a line of the Milky Way.
- Use pearls and buttons for moons and planets in the distance.
- When finished, fold the edges of the material over the ends of the board and glue down on the back.

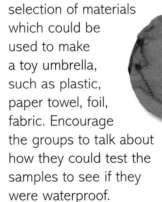

explore what would be the best material for a teddy's umbrella. Give each group a selection of materials which could be used to make a toy umbrella, such as plastic, paper towel, foil, fabric. Encourage the groups to talk about how they could test the samples to see if they were waterproof.
- **Literacy** – Play the game 'Twenty Questions', the children have to guess which object you have taken out of the bag by asking questions such as 'Is it heavy?' When it becomes clear from the questions they have guessed the object, someone can give the answer.

Looking at Pictures

This theme allows children to explore issues or events in their lives. It can consist of current issues such as recycling or pictures from books or artists that fit into whatever topic the class may be following. This theme will develop the children's observation skills by encouraging them to look carefully and record what they see.

Tropical Forest

- Henri Rousseau (1844–1910) was a French Post-Impressionist painter. His best-known paintings depict jungle scenes, even though he never left France or saw a jungle. His inspiration came from the botanical gardens in Paris and stuffed animals. His work was very tidy, yet exaggerated, with all the different parts brought carefully together.
- Look at Rousseau's painting *Tropical Forest with Monkeys* (1910). Discuss the picture. Do the children notice that the flowers are bigger than the monkeys' heads? Draw attention to the light and dark greens used and how the picture seems very well organised with groups of leaves in set places.
- Pre-cut a copy of the painting into twelve equal pieces. Explain to the children that they are going to work on just one part of the picture but that all the pieces will be put together at the end like a jigsaw to make one big picture.
- In pairs, ask the children to paint their own section of the painting. They will need to mix paints to match the colours in the painting. Give each pair a piece of paper about 40 cm by 40 cm, two mixing palettes and some water pots. One palette will need a few basic colours such as green, white, black, brown and yellow; the other palette can be used for mixing colours. Those children with some sky in their section will need blue, while others with the red leaves will need to add red to their palettes.
- Begin by asking the children to identify the lightest green or blue in the picture and encourage them to cover the paper with the light watery green so they start with the background and gradually add on the detail.

Viewfinder

What can you see?

We began by covering most of the picture and trying to imagine what the picture might be about. We gradually uncovered more and more of the picture, until we could see it all.

We looked through the viewfinder and chose a section of the picture to draw.

Exotic Landscape (1910) By Henri Rousseau

- This activity can easily be linked to whatever topic you may be following.
- Begin by covering most of a picture, such as *Exotic Landscape* by Henri Rousseau, with pieces of card and leaving just a small square centimetre showing. Ask the children what they think this picture might be, encouraging all suggestions. Gradually expand the area that the children can see and discuss their ideas as the picture becomes clearer the more it is revealed. Discuss the style of painting. Do they recognise it? Have they seen this type of painting before?
- Read the children a text about the picture – for example, *Jungle Book* by Doris Kutshback (Prestel, 2005), which discusses Rousseau's style of painting.
- Provide viewfinders and a piece of card or plastic with a centimetre square hole in the middle for the children to look through. Invite the children to look through their viewfinders and choose a part of the painting they would like to replicate. It can be a corner 4 cm by 4 cm or a smaller square of the painting.
- Discuss with the children how they are going to draw the section of the whole painting with the same amount of detail as if they were taking a photo.
- Provide colouring pencils and a piece of cartridge paper about 10 cm by 10 cm.

Encourage the children to look very closely at the part of the picture they are drawing. This activity will develop their observational skills as they will have to draw everything within the snapshot of the picture.

Cross-curricular Links

- **Literacy** – Use books to investigate an animal from the jungle. Form a question that the children would like to answer and use books to find that answer. Use knowledge gained from the investigation and a thesaurus to extend key words to describe the animal.
  - Read *Rumble in the Jungle* by Giles Andreae (Orchard, 2000). Discuss the poem and the different animals described in each verse. Use this as a model for a team poem in which each team member chooses an animal and creates a verse of four lines. Invite the children to perform their poems to the class.
- **Drama/Literacy** – Organise a drama group to come in and support the work you are doing on jungles. They could stimulate role playing by telling the story of a journey through the jungle. Then ask the children to write a postcard about their journey through the jungle. Encourage them to concentrate on their senses and feelings and to focus on adjectives and descriptive vocabulary.

Rubbish Tip

- Before starting this activity, invite the children to collect some rubbish. Specific items to collect are: plastic bottles of various sizes and colours; boxes used for packaging of various sizes; plastic bags of different colours; and wrappings such as fun-packs of chocolate bars or large packets of crisps.
- Begin by reading *Making a Difference Reducing Rubbish* by Sue Barraclough (Franklin Watts, 2006). Encourage the children to contribute their ideas about recycling and what they can do to help.
- Cut out a rubbish tip as large as the display board can manage, then cut the paper into three sections. Each section can be used to stick one of the three different types of rubbish you have collected. When each piece is covered then put another layer on top to give the work depth. Try to put things at different angles and mix it up with interesting colours.
- These pieces will take a while to dry and then they can be arranged together to look like a rubbish tip. Arrange signs with information about recycling around the tip to encourage conversion and sharing ideas about the topic.
- Paint some large seagulls that can be arranged around the tip to give it a realistic yet humorous look.

Pastel Collage

- Following on from work on recycling and rubbish tips, discuss with the children the range of rubbish tips you can find – cars, plastic bottles and general rubbish. Explore how goods get to a rubbish tip and what happens to them.
- Provide the children with a piece of A3 coloured sugar paper and some pastels.
- In pairs, ask the children to draw a part of a tip or the whole tip in pastels, concentrating on

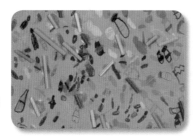

just one type of rubbish or a variety.
- When the drawing is finished, provide the children with items you have collected, such as nuts and bolts, screws, straws, springs and small boxes to use as a collage on their work. If a child has drawn cars on the tip, then lots of metal pieces will complement their work, while cut up plastic straws will look great on a bottle bank.
- This work could be displayed on its own or at the side of the large rubbish collage.

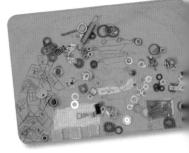

Around Our School

- Children love this activity because they have the opportunity to use a camera. Send groups around the school, playground or local area, with an adult, to take a photo of something they would like to paint.
- This activity links in well with geography topics exploring the school and the local area. It can also fit in with a rubbish topic and the children can compare tidy areas with areas where rubbish has been thrown or where there are overflowing bins.
- Print out the photos and have them ready for the following week. Provide the children with their photo, paint and coloured A3 sugar paper.

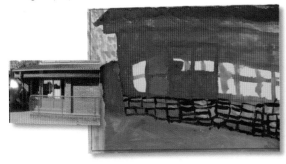

- As a class, look closely at several of the photos and discuss the detail. Demonstrate beginning with the background so detail can be added to give a feeling of depth.
- Ask the children to copy the photo very carefully. This will develop their observation skills and fine motor control.

Cross-curricular Links

- **Art** – Sort materials that can be recycled or reused. Complete a drawing of items that can be recycled and those that cannot. Discuss ways the children can reduce rubbish.
- **Geography** – Concentrate on environmental issues, such as dealing with rubbish. We do not have enough room to carry on burying huge amounts of rubbish in landfill sites. What can the children do to help?
- **PSHCE** – Explore many of the reasons why we should recycle. Begin by looking at school and home. What is in the children's lunchbox? What could they recycle at school? Did they know they can raise money for the school or charity by simply recycling? Some businesses will pay for aluminium cans and foil.

Homes

This theme is very familiar and children will be able to recognise and talk about some characteristics of home and home life. They will have the opportunity to identify different types of homes, such as caravans and flats. By walking around their locality, the children will notice differences and similarities between homes as well as recognise familiar features found in different types of houses, such as windows and chimneys. This theme has great cross-curricular links especially to geography, history and literacy.

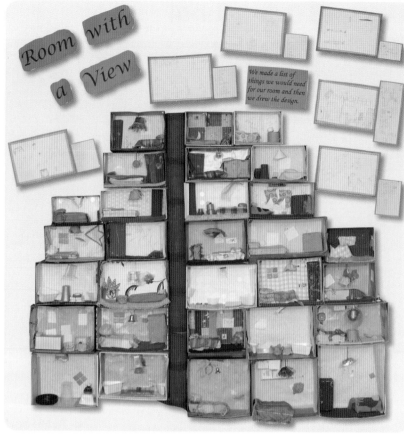

Rooms in Cardboard Boxes

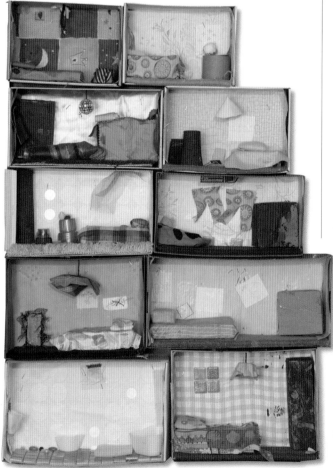

- Discuss with the children the different rooms in their house and what the function is of each. What is special about a kitchen or a lounge?
- Invite the children to make any room they like – their bedrooms will be a favourite.
- Provide, or ask the children to bring in, a shoebox, some wallpaper, tiles, materials, carpet and small boxes for furniture.
- Ask the children to decide what to put on the walls (wallpaper or tiles) and on the floor (carpet, tiles or wood effect). Decorating the walls and the floor can be the aim for one session.
- Next, ask the children to make small pieces of furniture, such as a bed from a matchbox covered with material or a light hanging from the ceiling with a lid and string. Shiny paper can be used as a mirror and little pictures can be drawn or cut out from cards to make pictures to hang on the wall. Make windows that the children can hang material around for curtains. The children will have lots of ideas, so make sure you have lots of little boxes and lids for them to use.
- Invite the children to add some Lego® or Playmobil® people to their rooms.

Photos of Homes

- After a walk around the local area, discuss the different types of homes that the children saw – terraced, detached, flats etc – and encourage the children to bring in a photo of their homes. Talk about the various parts of a building such as roofs, windows and types of bricks. Draw attention to the main shapes that the children can identify in their photos.

- Demonstrate painting a house starting with the main shapes – for example, a rectangle for the house and triangles for the roof and porch. Encourage the children to look closely at their photos. How many windows are there and on what side is the door?

- Provide the children with:
  – an A3 piece of cartridge paper and a mixing palette containing the main colours;
  – a spare mixing palette so they can make extra colours and different shades of colour;
  – a range of paintbrushes in different thicknesses.
  – a pot of water to clean their paintbrush and encourage them to change the water themselves when necessary.

- Talk to the children while they are painting and draw attention to different aspects of the homes, encouraging them to add detail such as bricks.

- Display the paintings with a map of the area identifying local landmarks that the children will have seen in their walk.

Cross-curricular Links

- **Outdoor Adventure Activity** – Take the children for a walk around the local area and look at different types of homes. The children can draw the different types of homes seen, labelling the main features, door, window, wall, chimney, etc. Visiting local shops can be made interesting by talking to the local shopkeepers before the walk; they may do some special things. A baker may make little buns for the children and show them around the shop; a carpet shop may give the children little samples of carpet for the rooms they are making.

- **Geography** – Use a map of the local area and a Google Earth map of the area. Encourage the children to describe the features of the local environment and the different types of houses.

- **Literacy** – Ask the children to write a list of the items they need to decorate the room in their box. They need to decide which room they are going to make and what to put on the floors and walls. Start by drawing a picture and then write a list of materials to make the furniture and to decorate their room.

- **Science** – Using 2D and 3D materials, invite the children to experiment with joining in different ways – hinges, staples, treasury tags, glue, tape.

The Three Pigs

- The story of the three pigs lends itself well to the discussion of different types of homes and the material from which they are built. Read the story to the class then invite the children to retell the story and act it out in groups.
- Writing this story may take a couple of days, so while working on the story organise some groups to begin a collage for the background.
  - Create the sky with strips of blue crepe paper and sponge print with white, light blue and dark blue paint.
  - Print the grass by rolling marbles over paint poured onto the paper. Pour different shades of green and a little yellow on green sugar paper, then roll the marbles over the paper. When the rolling is finish, give the children a piece of paper to create a few flowers by printing with different colours using the end of a thick pencil.
  - Print a simple path on yellow or brown

sugar paper with wooden printing blocks using brown, yellow or gold paint.
- The three pigs' houses need to be large. Collect some sticks, straw and bricks to make the display look more realistic. Invite some children to paint on the doors and then ask everyone to glue on the sticks and straw – make sure you use plenty of glue. Create the collage of the brick house with red and brown brick-shaped tissue paper. Collect a few house bricks to display in front of the house.
- Cut out the pigs collage with different shades of pink tissue and crepe paper.
- Create the wolf with fur and brown/gold crepe fringing to give him a hairy appearance.
- Invite the children to suggest speech bubbles for the various characters. This can lead to interesting conversations about the characters profiles, showing how the pigs may be feeling and what they can do to help each other.

Three Pigs Painted Windows

- Ask the children to sponge print a background of sky and land for the pictures. They may need to stand on tables to reach the top of the windows, so provide appropriate supervision.
- Depending on the age of the children, an adult may need to outline the pigs and the houses for

the children to paint. Display the books the children have written about the story around the painted windows.

Happy Homes

Friedensreich (born Friedrich) Hundertwasser (1928–2000) was an Austrian painter and sculptor. Common themes found in his work include the rejection of straight lines and use of bright colours. Colour was very important to him and he felt heaven must be a colourful, bright place. He always framed his pictures in black as he thought it made the colours shine like jewels. He believed that if people lived in bright and cheerful homes, they would have happier and more interesting lives.

- Look at Hundertwasser's *637A Waiting Houses* (1969). This is a good example of his use of colour and lack of straight lines.
- In pairs, provide the children with an A3 piece of sugar paper and some brightly coloured paints. Give pair a piece of scrap paper and ask them to discuss and then sketch their ideas. This does not need to be detailed and once their ideas are clear, they can paint together, working on separate parts. Encourage the children to talk about their work and add detail to the buildings.
- Allow the painting to dry and then cut out the houses. Ask the children to add some collage to their work using sequins, shiny paper and special jewels. Provide some scissors for them to cut out the shapes.

Cross-curricular Links

- **Science** – Build three houses, one with Lego® bricks, one with sticks and the other with straw. When you have the different types of houses, test the structures with a hairdryer (the Wolf) and see which is the strongest.
- **Literacy** – Read the story of the three pigs and introduce the idea of a story having the structure of a beginning, a middle and an end. Use different coloured paper to illustrate the three parts of a story.
  - Make a book by writing about the story of the three pigs.
  - Write an alternative ending to the three pigs story.
  - Make a 'wanted' poster for Mr Wolf or a writing activity 'Have you seen this wolf?' Structure the sheet with boxes with different headings. What does he look like? What is he wearing? Why is he dangerous? What bad deeds has be done?

Light and Dark

In this theme the children will have the opportunity to explore the effect of light and dark shades of colour and the need for light to see. They will work with light and dark colours and explore how they work together. They will also see the relationship between light, an object and the formation of shadows.

Sunset on the Isle of Struay.

Marbling Silhouettes

- Arrange for the children to prepare their marbling sheets a week before the lesson so they are dry to work on.
- Provide a tray large enough to take a piece of A3 paper. Put about a centimetre of water in the tray and add a little vinegar.
- Use a pipette to put plenty of marbling ink onto the water. The marbling ink will float on the water.
- Gently place the paper onto the water. The ink will print onto the paper quickly. Remove the paper from the tray and allow to dry.

- This activity lends itself to many topics and books that might be used in class. This example is based on the *Katie Morag* series by Mairi Hedderwick (Random House, 1997–2011). After reading the books, ask the children choose a part of the island they would like to silhouette against a sunset.
- Ask the children to cut out pieces of black sugar paper or card to stick onto the marbling. Encourage them to start with a main shape such as a lighthouse and some land formation so the picture has a focus point to work around, then add detail such as people, rocks and trees.

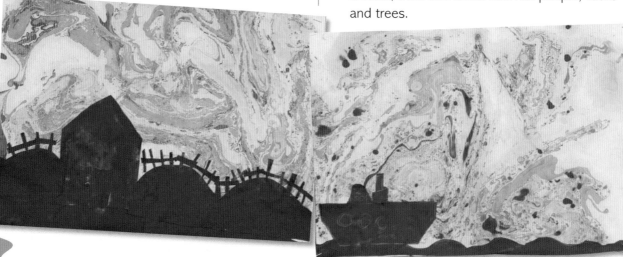

Collage Silhouettes

- Prepare by placing a sheet of A3 paper on a wall and positioning an overhead projector to shine on it. Stand a child between the projector and the paper. Arrange for an adult to carefully draw around the shadow of the child's head that appears on the paper. With young children, an adult needs to cut out the silhouette of the child because the fine details make the silhouette more recognisable.

- Explain to the children that they are going to make a mosaic of the silhouettes of their heads with cellophane, shiny paper or sweet wrappers.

- Ask the children to choose whether to work with a couple of colours or completely mix all the colours in the mosaic. Provide PVA glue. Stress that they only need a small amount and they should wipe the glue stick so it does not drip over their work because it is difficult to work if the mosaic becomes too sticky.

- When completely covered and dried, coat the heads with a thin layer of PVA glue to give a shiny finish. Mount the heads on black paper for a dramatic affect.

Cross-curricular Links

- **Science** – Create a dark area in the classroom and ask the children to find some objects. Gradually increase the light, introducing the idea that light is essential for seeing things. Give the children a black box with a small peephole in one end and a larger hole covered with cardboard in the top. Ask the children to explore what they can see when there is light and when there is no light.

  – Discuss the sources of light and make a collection comparing the light from different sources.

  – Invite the children to explore shadow formation using torches and overhead projectors.

  – On a bright sunny day, visit the school grounds to observe shadows – some may be formed by clouds. Ask the children to draw around shadows of themselves. Record their shadows in the morning and then later in the day.

- **Maths** – At different times of the day, measure and record the lengths of the shadow of a metre stick. Write the results in a table and construct a bar chart.

Light and Dark Faces

- Discuss portraits and self-portraits with the children. Use *What is a Self-Portrait?* by Ruth Thomson (Franklin Watts, 2005) as a stimulus. Many artists try to paint exactly what they see; however, Pablo Picasso (1881–1973) believed a work of art exists as an object in its own right, not merely as a record of reality. Look at the colours and shapes he used in *The Weeping Woman* (1937) – the painting shows the pain the young woman was feeling at that time.
- Provide A3 paper and coloured pencils.
- Explain to the children that they are going to draw a face and pay particular attention to the detail, but it does not have to be an exact image. They can use the faces of children at their table as a stimulus but they do not have to draw that person.
- One half of the face should be in dark strong colours, while the other side is coloured in light, gentle colours. This can be interpreted as dark blue on one side and light blue on the other side, using different shades of the same colours.

We experimented with **light and dark** shades on different sides of a face.

Picasso believed that a work of art exists as an object in its own right, not merely as a record of reality.

- Alternatively they may use dark colours on one side such as black, purple and blue, while using yellow, orange and white on the other side. Allow the children interpret this activity in their own way and they should produce some interesting results.

Changing Light to Dark

- Provide each child with a rectangular piece of paper and a mixing palette with a blob of white and blue paint in a well.
- Ask the children to paint a line in white on their paper. Next they need to dip their paintbrush in the tiniest bit of blue paint and mix into the white. The white paint will change its shade very slightly. They should paint a line in this colour next to the white colour. The line should be very slightly darker in colour.
- They should then add a little more blue and paint the result.

- Display the rectangles on top of each other like a ladder and use some strips of cellophane to give the display depth.

44

Light and Dark Perspective

- Artists can use lines to give a picture depth – this is called perspective. The artist uses a point in the distance of a picture, such as where a road disappears. This is called the vanishing point and the observer's eye is drawn to this point. Use *The Avenue at Middelharnis* (1689) by Meindert Hobbema (1638–1709) and *Saruwaka Cho Street* (1856) by Ando Hiroshige (1797–1858) to demonstrate this claim. If you run your finger along the lines of the street, you will find the vanishing point.
- Provide a range of white paper in sizes from A3 to 15 cm square and some black and white paints.

- Ask the children to draw five or six pencil lines coming out from one point at the top of their paper and running diagonally down the sheet. Next draw six lines running across the page.
- Ask the children to paint alternate squares with white paint and then add black paint to the remaining squares.

Stained Glass Window

- Use black card 14 cm by 20 cm and cut out an arch-shaped window in the centre.
- Give the children tissue paper or coloured cellophane in strips to stick across the window.

- Allow the strips to dry and then laminate the whole window, with a number stuck on the coloured section.
- Present the windows together in your classroom window for an effective display.

Buildings

This theme gives the children the opportunity to explore shape and pattern in buildings. Begin by looking at shape, space and pattern in local buildings. By looking at various paintings of buildings, the children will begin to notice different ways of drawing buildings – some with a lot of detail and others with little. They can explore and use shape, form, colour and pattern to design their own 3D town with buildings and local landmarks.

Cubism House

- Look at the work of Georges Braque (1882–1963) particularly *Viaduct at L'Estaque* (1908) and *Houses at L'Estaque* (1908), which demonstrate the Cubist style. Use *Art Revolutions Cubism* by Linda Bolton (Belitha Press, 2000) and *How Artists Use Shape* by Paul Flux (Heinemann, 2001) to demonstrate the style. The paintings are made up of little cubes. The landscape is not shown in a realistic way but is broken into bold cubic shapes. The buildings are solid shapes, broken up by light and shadow. Compare this style with *The Hay Wain* (1821) by John Constable (1776–1837) where the artist has painted the picture with lots of attention, which can be seen in the detail on the roof.

- After reading about the artist and talking about the Cubist style, demonstrate how to draw a house. Begin by showing the children how a house is normally drawn – a square with a door and four windows, a roof and chimney. This will appear very flat, so draw a 3D building. Start with a simple cube shape and omit detail such as bricks. Fill in the sides using blocks of earth colours.

- Give each child a piece of A3 white paper and a tray of water colours. Ask them to paint 3D buildings keeping the shapes simple.

- Encourage them to paint the sides of the buildings with blocks of earth colours that they can blend and mix with their watercolours.

- Add the trees and background after the Cubist house shapes are finished. Discuss not always placing the trees at the side of the buildings because this makes the painting very flat. Explain that putting the trees or bushes behind or in front of the house will give the painting more depth. Demonstrate this on the board to give the children a visual aid.

Papier Mâché Buildings

- Read *The Big Katie Morag Storybook* by Mairi Hedderwick (Red Fox, 2000). This is a story of a little girl living on a Scottish island. Discuss where the different characters live and the type of landscape around the island.
- In pairs, ask the children to make a 3D model of part of the island. They can choose to make a model of the Post Office, Grannie's House, the Lighthouse, Castle McColl, the Mews Cottages or any building that catches their imagination.
- Provide a piece of board or firm card and a variety of boxes, tubes and lids to give the model structure.
- Ask the children to stick small cereal boxes to the board with masking tape, and add lids and cardboard tubes to give shape for the garden or edge of the water line.
  A tube cut in half long ways and taped onto the board makes a good jetty for the boats to moor at in the harbour.
- When the children have enough structure, ask them to papier mâché the whole board. Use torn strips of newspaper dipped in cellulose glue to completely cover the boxes and base of the board. Use flat hands to rub over the structure to make it smooth in order to show the outline of the buildings.
- Allow several days to dry before painting and adding detail on the model. Encourage the children to bring in items they would like to add to their model such as rocks, stones, sand, plastic flowers. Use plenty of glue to stick these pieces. Use thick paint to cover the newspaper, starting with the grass,

houses and the sea. Encourage the children to use different shades of colour for the sea and the landscape to make it look more interesting. Then add the finer detail onto the roof and windows.

Cross-curricular Links

- **Geography** – Locate Scotland and the Western Isles on a map of the United Kingdom. Use atlases, maps and globes to locate and name the countries of the United Kingdom, label the main cities, rivers and oceans around the country.
  - Draw a map of the Isle of Struay, labelling its main physical and human features. Mark on the places mentioned in the story such as Grannie's House, Boggy Loch, the Castle, the Lighthouses and the Post Office.
  - With the help of pictures and photographs, compare the physical and human features with the children's local environment. Look for similarities' and differences between the two localities.
- **Drama** – Role play pretending to be characters from the island and describe their day. Consider what life is like on the island, such as the ferry arriving three times a week to bring all the items the islanders need. How does this compare with life in the children's local town?

Reflective Paintings

- Make a list of different buildings with the children from lighthouses and pyramids to huts and skyscrapers.
- Provide A3 white paper, oil pastels and watercolours.
- Decide whether to work in landscape or portrait and then draw a line just under half-way across the sheet.
- Demonstrate using pastels to draw across the top half of the paper. The children will need to add lots of detail and completely fill the top half of the sheet.

- This activity takes a while to complete and the second part of the drawing is better done as a separate activity.
- Next the children should paint a reflection of the building in water using watercolour paints. As the building is reflected in the water, it will be upside down and this will require concentration and skill.
- Encourage the children to keep their brush wet – it does not matter if some of the colours run into each other because it is a reflection and the lines would be blurred.

Buildings in Clay

- Discuss with children different types of buildings and their shapes, such as a Lighthouse or a Cottage.
- Provide a piece of clay, a rolling pin, a board, and some cutting tools. Roll out the clay to between half a centimetre and a centimetre thickness. Cut out the shape and put the spare bits of clay to the side to use later on the front of the building.
- Provide forks and other tools to make markings on the buildings. Potato mashers are useful for this. Ask the children to roll the spare pieces of clay and put around doors and windows to add detail.
- Explain that the buildings will be displayed flat on pieces of black card, so they will just be seen from the front.

- When finished, stick the building onto a piece of card, then coat with watered down glue to give it a shiny finish.
- Allow buildings time to dry, then paint with metallic silver, gold or copper paint.

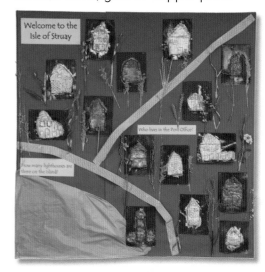

War Picture

- Look at the work of Naïve artists, particularly Mister Denham (1946–2003) – for example, his *Landscape with Distraction*. He founded the British Naïves in 2000, which was made up of ordinary people with no art training. Their pictures tell a story about real life using landscape, architecture and people. They are less concerned with perspective, scale or realism and far more interested in the story or events and their details.

- The main picture above was produced as part of a topic on World War Two. Before beginning the picture, it is useful if the children have gained some knowledge about the period, then their drawings can better represent the time.

- Explain that the picture will be built up in layers, with each piece being cut out and glued to the board. Ask the children to start with small pieces of grey paper and draw and then cut out roof outlines only.

- Next using slightly larger pieces of grey paper, they should cut out building shapes and add a little detail in pencil. These should be layered in front of the roof outlines.

- They can then draw the buildings and shops on slightly larger pieces of coloured paper. They can place their buildings on the board, layering the picture and gradually working downwards. Finally, they should then add people and aircraft.

Cross-curricular Links

- **Outdoor Adventure Activity** – Walk around the local area making a list of the buildings the children see. Describe the different types of building and compare them to those from pictures taken during the war.

Habitats

This theme helps children to learn about plants and animals in their immediate environment. They should observe minibeasts and animals in their natural environments through walks and visits to centres that run visits for children. The children should have plenty of opportunity to make observations, measure and make comparisons, and present their findings in drawings and graphs, using the results to develop their knowledge.

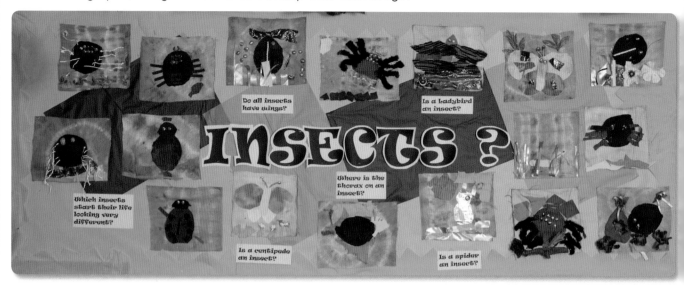

Tie-Dye Insect Collages

- Collect some plain white cotton sheets to cut into approximately 25 cm squares and make a collection of thick rubber bands. Create some tie-dyed squares by holding one piece of material and tying a rubber band around the held end. Go over the same spot repeatedly so the die cannot seep beneath the band. Tie another rubber band further down – when cut off, this will produce circles of white ripples from the centre. Another way to tie-dye is to fold the material like a concertina, zigzagging back and forth. Fold the ends over and tie with a rubber band in a couple of places. Dip the material with the rubber band ties in a cold water dye. Remove material from the dye, leave until they have stopped dripping, then cut off the rubber bands. When dry, iron the pieces of material to make them flat.

- Ask the children to decide which insect they would like to make a collage of and then draw it on some felt and cut it out.
- Ask the children to stick the insect onto the tie-dye material and use other materials to collage the insect, such as shiny circles for butterfly wings, ribbons and interesting papers.
- A collection of stones, sand, flowers and beads are useful for collage work. These can be used to show where the insects live in their habitats. Invite the children to bring in individual pieces for their collage as this encourages interest in their work.

Clay Insects

- Provide the children with several pieces of clay. An insect has three body parts, so three pieces would be a good idea if making an ant for example.
- Ask the children to mould the clay into the shapes required and gently pinch the pieces together.
- When they are happy with the shape, use wire to add wings, legs or antennae to the model.

Cross-curricular Links

- **Science** – Walk around the local environment and a pond area and learn the names of the some of the plants and animals. Notice where some of the animals and insects are found – do they have different habitats? How many different types of habitats can the children identify and what animals would they expect to find in them?
  - Complete an animal survey answering questions such as: 1) Does it fly, swim, walk? 2) Does it have a shell, wings, feathers? 3) How many legs does it have? 4) Did you find it on its own?
  - Collect insects in special specimen jars and closely observe the different parts of their body. How many legs do they have and how many main body parts do they have? Label the body parts of an insect.
  - Investigate different habitats such as open grassy fields, woodlands, under a log, a bush, the edge of a pond, around a tree and the playground. Notice what animals and plants live there and whether it is wet or dry, sunny or shady, windy or sheltered.
  - Investigate the life around a pond or life under and around a stone and record what plants and animals are found there.
  - Keep a minibeast record chart for several weeks. Record where the minbeasts were found, how many legs they have, how they travel, etc. Then complete a flow diagram to help decide whether the minibeast is an insect, an arachnid, a crustacean or mollusc.
  - Compare the life cycles of frogs, caterpillars and birds.

Habitat Display

- Discuss with the children the different kinds of habitats where animals and insects live. Brainstorm a list of habitats that could be included in the display.

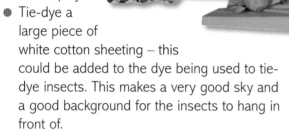

- Tie-dye a large piece of white cotton sheeting – this could be added to the dye being used to tie-dye insects. This makes a very good sky and a good background for the insects to hang in front of.
- Sponge-print some large pieces of green sugar paper with various shades of paint. Add some brown sponge-printed areas for mud and soil, which are habitats for some animals.
- Make a tree by painting a large tube in brown colours, then tear strips of tissue to stick on as bark. Cut out and paint some branches on which to stick tissue leaves.
- Long grass – cut some strips of green sugar paper and paint them.
- Long grass – cut some strips of green sugar paper and paint them.
- Ant hill – cut out dome shapes and paint with brown paint mixed with sand and glue. When finished, sprinkle with more sand.
- Flowers – cut out circles that can be decorated around the edge with crepe petals and put lentils and seeds in the middle.
- Logs – make a collection of sticks. Tie some together and attach to the wall with a staple gun. Fix some sticks on brown pieces of sugar paper using plenty of glue.

Papier Mâché Insects

- Explain to the children that they will be making some papier mâché insects to hang in front of a habitats display.
- Give each child a balloon to blow up. Long thin balloons are good for butterflies and dragonflies, while round balloons make good ladybirds and bees. Use thin wire for butterfly wings by making two circles of wire taped together and stuck onto the balloon. The newspaper can cover the wire where it is attached – add several layers to secure.
- Tear plenty of newspaper into strips and mix the cellulose paste with cold water. Ask the children to dip the paper into the paste and cover their balloon. They should keep adding strips in all directions, covering the balloon with several layers. If only one layer is used, when the balloon dries and deflates the newspaper will sink down. Three layers should be enough for the newspaper to keep its shape.
- When enough layers have been put on, ask the children to smooth the surface with their hands to create an even finish so the insects will be easier to paint.
- After several days the insects will be dry. The children can then paint their insect – bees will have yellow and black stripes; ladybirds can be red and with black spots; spiders may be black or tarantulas can have fringed tissue paper to make them hairy.
- Body parts can be added when dry, such as legs for grasshoppers and spiders, buttons for eyes and pipe cleaners for antenna.

Joan Miro Insects

Joan Miró (1893–1983) was a Spanish painter and sculptor. His work is considered to be Surrealist. He expressed contempt for conventional painting methods and wanted to recreate a child-like form with an element of surprise that was simplistic.

- Look at some of Miro's paintings showing birds and insects. Ask the children to note the colours and shapes he used and how he painted them. The drawings are very simple and not realistic. Talk to the children about drawing, for instance, a butterfly in an imaginative way, using the body parts of other insects instead.
- Stick together enough paper to create the background for the display. Invite groups of children to sponge paint this paper with different shades of blue while working on their creatures.
- Provide each child with a piece of blue sugar paper or card to paint a black outline of their creature. Encourage them to develop their ideas and be as creative as possible – the different parts of the creature can be made up of different insects or birds or animals. Their creature may be a ladybird's body with butterfly wings or a duck's head and a cat's tail. Discuss the different ideas so the children understand they can be as imaginative as they like.
- When they have painted the outline in black, ask them to colour the creature. Provide a limited range of colours – white, green, red, blue and yellow. The whole creature does not need to be painted in colour – for example, half a head and half a body can be red while the other half may just be white.
- When the creatures are dry, cut them out and arrange them on the blue sponge-printed paper and glue them on. Display as one large collage.

Cross-curricular Links

- **Literacy** – Create a simple minibeast wordsearch for the children to find the names of different minibeasts in the block of letters. Then give the children a 10cm by 10cm grid and ask them to create their own wordsearch for their friends to complete.
- **ICT/Literacy** – The children could create their own minibeast quiz using the facts about minibeasts they have learned during this theme. Encourage them to use non-fiction books to extend their knowledge and the depth of their questions. Their questions can be typed up on the computer and displayed for other children to answer.
- **ICT/Maths** – Complete a minibeast survey and record the results on a graph and table to be analysed. The results can be put onto the computer using a simple data-handling program such as *2 Count* and *2 Graph* by 2 Simple Software.

People and Faces

A face is one of the first things we learn to recognise with our eyes. We learn to understand what the expression on people's faces mean – angry, sad, happy or unsure. When children first make a picture of a face, it is probably just a circle, with dots for eyes and lines for the nose and mouth. This theme gives the opportunity to explore facial images through collage, photos, papier mâché and mosaic.

Distorted Collage

David Hockney (b. 1937) is one of the most famous British artists of the 20th century. He became reknowned as a painter before turning his attention to photography. As a photographer, Hockney's work is often an odd sort of photo montage – a giant image made up of many smaller photographs. Introduce the children to his photographic collage *Mother I* (1985). He has rearranged the photo altering the whole impression that it gives.

- Explain to the children that they are going to explore an image of themselves and distort it by cutting it up.
- Before starting this activity, take a photo of all the children. These can be printed out on a computer (20 cm by 15 cm is a useful size) or professionally developed.
- Provide a piece of card a little larger than the photo on which the children can make their collage.
- Provide the children with some wrapping paper to tear into the pieces they want to use. They should stick these onto the card, overlapping them to completely cover the card and give a layered and textured finished to the collage. Encourage the children to work with shades of the same colour. When finished, allow the cards to dry.
- Discuss ideas with the children for how to cut their photo. Diagonally and zigzag are all good opinions but encourage them to experiment and try different approaches. They can then cut up their photo and arrange it on the collage. When they are happy with the arrangement, they should stick the pieces onto the collage.

Jawlensky Portraits

- Alexej Georgewitsch von Jawlensky (1864–1941) was a Russian expressionist painter who studied and worked in Germany. Jawlensky used colours and shapes to produce a mood or feeling rather than to describe a real face. Look at his portraits *Abstract Head* (c.1928) – he painted several different versions with the same name. Discuss the abstract nature of the paintings. Is it clear that it is a head or could it be something else?
- Provide the children with watercolours and a piece of A3 sugar paper.
- Ask them to think about the shades they would like to use that may convey a mood. If their abstract painting has an angry mood, they may want to use reds and purples. Interestingly, children's views on which colours convey certain moods can vary, so allow them to explore their ideas.
- They should begin by mixing shades of colours and thinly painting them in shapes onto the page. Gradually they can cover the whole page with blocks of colour – it does not matter if the shades of colour run into each other and the blocks do not need to be uniform shape or size.
- Provide a selection of different-sized paintbrushes so the children can chose the appropriate size of paintbrush to paint their face. Then they can begin to paint parts of the face – a simple wavy line may be enough for the hair on the side of the face.
- Encourage them to use colours that complement the shades they have used for the background and to experiment with different shapes and lines for the eyes.

Cross-curricular Links

- **Art** – Examples of Pop Art by Andy Warhol (1928–87) would give ideas to the children to make printing blocks for faces of different colours. This technique would be similar to leaf printing on page 11.
  - Do some close observational drawings. Encourage the children to look in mirrors at their own faces, noting how far down their face their eyes are in relation to their nose, etc and the shape of their eyes and mouth. It is important to encourage them to examine the details of their face before beginning more abstract work.
- **Literacy** – Look at some poetry that examines feelings and moods linked to colours to support work on people and faces.

Clay Faces

- Give each child a piece of clay to roll out with a rolling pin until approximately 1 cm thick. Provide a circular shape as a template. Ask the children to cut around the circle with a knife and place the extra pieces to one side so they can be used later.
- Ask the children to begin by making the features for the face – the eyes can be rolled and flattened slightly when put on the face. Encourage them to think about the shape of a nose, squeezing and pinching the clay until they are happy with the shape.
- When adding bits such as the mouth, they should make sure the clay is pressed into the face to help it stay on. Hair can be added last.
- Allow the faces to dry and then invite the children to paint them with thick paint, carefully giving the features different colours to make them stand out.

- Display on material such as hessian using all the faces created by the class.

Mosaic Papier Mâché Faces

- Begin by discussing the features of a face. Provide each child with a large paper plate, lids, corks and shapes to cover with papier mâché using strips of newspaper.
- Ask the children to attach the corks or folded card with masking tape to the plate. It does not matter what this looks like because it will all be covered but encourage the children to spread out the features so they can be distinguished when covered. Ensure the children use lids that are large enough because when they are covered, they can disappear if the pieces are too small such as buttons.
- When the features have been attached, the children should cover the plate completely with strips of newspaper dipped in cellulose water glue. They should use at least two layers and keep smoothing the newspaper down with their hands.
- The face should be left to dry for at least a few days.

- Invite the children to cover the face with pre-cut pieces of paper, concentrating on certain colours and using cut tissue and shiny, crepe and see-through paper in that colour. Purples and orange can look very striking together.
- Encourage the children to smoothe down the paper as they cover the faces and then apply a thin layer of PVA glue to give it a shiny finished look.
- The faces may need to be trimmed around the edge to make a tidy finish.

Tribal Masks

Masks are common in cultures all around the world and throughout history. Different cultures use masks as part of cultural rituals — performing, dancing, playing and transforming the person. Begin by looking at the *Tribal Mask of Benin* (16th century) from West Africa. It is an idealised representation of female beauty, believed to be a portrait of Queen Idia, mother of King Esigie who ruled Benin in the 16th century.

- In preparation for this activity, involve the children in collecting a variety of masks and images from Africa.
- Discuss with the children what the masks are made from and where they may come from — for example, Egyptian masks are very distinctive. Ask them to consider the different shapes and who the masks might have been made for. Invite them to look closely at the details, which have often been carved into the wood and are very intricate.
- Provide large pieces of sugar paper, charcoal and a putty eraser.
- Ask the children to begin by using very gentle lines to copy the shape of the mask. Demonstrate how to smudge the charcoal with fingers or paper towels to shade the different areas of the mask. If the lines become rubbed out, then the children can go over them with firmer lines.
- The children can use the putty eraser to remove lines they do not like and to clean up areas which may have been smudged. They should concentrate on the detail and keep adding until they are satisfied with the result.

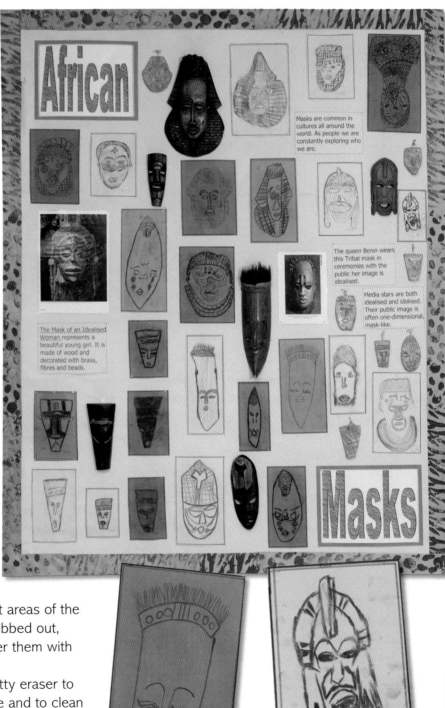

Water

This is an interesting theme where the children learn about the importance of clean water and investigate how it is supplied. They can contrast water use at home with use in less economically developed countries. About 450 million people today face water shortages, but people in rich countries are wasting it. We are used to turning on the tap and having fresh, running water whenever we want it. This theme lends itself well to increasing the children's knowledge of global issues and environmental responsibility.

The Great Wave of Kanagawa

Around 1830 Hokusai began to produce a series of woodcuts which show the sacred mountain of Japan, Mount Fuji.

In this scene the snow covered mountains can be seen in the far distance while the Great Wave dominates the picture.

The wave and sea are stylised, both in colour and shape, giving the print a flat, decorative character.

The Great Wave

- Katsushika Hokusai (1760–1849) was a Japanese painter and printmaker. Around 1830, Hokusai began to produce a series of woodcuts showing the sacred mountain of Japan, Mount Fuji, in 36 different views. Look at the painting *In the Well of the Great Wave off Kanagawa* (1829–32), the snow covered mountain can be seen in the far distance while the main subject of the picture is the great wave. The wave itself and the surrounding sea are stylised.
- Begin by asking the children to bubble print the sky with a very light blue paint. They can do this by mixing a little paint with water and washing up liquid, blowing into the pot and allowing the bubbles to run over the side and printing onto A5 pieces of white paper.
- Divide the sea into nine overlapping sections: three along the bottom, three along the middle and three along the top of the sea. Some will be bigger than others. Number them on the back 1 to 9.

- Sections 1, 3, 5, 7 and 9 will be covered with torn pieces of embossed wallpaper from a roll. Ask the children to paint the pieces of torn paper with various shades of blue paint, then stick them onto Section 1, starting from the top so the painted pieces can be overlapped and continuing to the bottom of the section.
- Sections 2, 4, 6 and 8 can be covered with torn strips of blue tissue, crepe and shiny paper. When the children have completely covered these, dab some thin PVA glue over all the tissue paper to give a shiny finish.
- Mount Fuji can be painted blue and white, with some thick white paint on the top to give the snow a textured appearance.
- The piece will need to be reconstructed carefully following the picture of the wave.

Under Water Squares

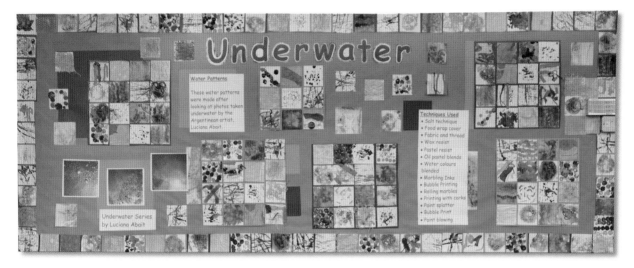

- Look at photos taken underwater by the Argentinean artist Luciana Abait (b. 1971) called *The Underwater Series* (2007). Discuss with the children the different ways they could show underwater pictures, drawing on many of the different techniques they have used in the past. Compile a list and ask the children to explore and experiment with the different techniques.
- Pre-cut an adequate number of 10 cm squares of white paper so that the children can try a variety of the following techniques:
- Salt technique – paint using shades of blue paint and sprinkle with salt.
- Foodwrap cover – paint a pattern with shades of blue paint and cover with clear food wrap before it dries; press down leave to dry and then peel off.
- Fabric and thread – provide a range of wool, thread and fabric and ask the children to arrange in circles or wavy shapes.
- Wax resist – using white wax crayons, make a pattern on paper and then cover with blue food colouring.
- Pastel resist – using blue and green pastels, design patterns and cover with food colouring.
- Oil pastel blends – using a range of blue and green pastels, blend shades of colour

into each other and then drag a paper towel across the pastels in wavy shapes to spread the colours together.
- Water colours – blend and mix to make a range of shades.
- Rolling marbles – place marbles in different shades of blue paint, then put in a tray with squares of paper and roll them over the paper.
- Paint splatter – gently tap the end of a paintbrush with paint on it.
- Display by putting mixed combinations of the squares together mounted on blue backing paper and use some squares as a border.

Cross-curricular Links

- **Maths** – Ask the children to record when they use water during the day/week. They should work out how much water they used and enter the data onto a spreadsheet on the computer. Can they work out how much they would use in a year?
  – Work out the amount of water used in the class on a particular day. Can the children work out how much is used in a week? They can then make suggestions for how to cut back on water usage.

Circle Weaving

- Provide 20 cm (or larger) firm paper plates, string in blue and greens if possible, and a collection of blue, silver, white and green wool with different textures to weave with.
- Pre-cut each plate with 12 indents around the rim to wind the string around – this will be the warp to weave the wool through.
- Pre-cut numerous pieces of wool about 40–50 cm long so the children can work independently on the activity.
- Explain to the children that they need to start at the centre of the plate where all the warps cross and tie the first piece of wool to the middle, then start weaving under and over gradually making a bigger circle as the wool expands out.
- When they reach the end of the piece of wool, they should tuck it under the wool that has been woven and then tie a new piece to the warp where the other one ended. Encourage them to change colours each time and build up the colours and texture they like.
- They should keep weaving until the paper plate is full. This activity will take several days, so it can be planned over several weeks.

Large Loose Weaving

- Provide some net curtains or material with some holes big enough to weave pieces of material and cord through. Involve the children in collecting material, wool and ribbons in sea colours such as blue, white, green, silver and purples.
- For this activity, it is useful to fasten the net curtain to a wall so groups of children can work on this over time. Put a box of pre-cut material, ribbon and needles by the hanging so the children can weave after finishing the work or as a group activity.
- Cut the material into thin strips that can be passed through some of the holes.
- Provide tapestry needles with large eyes so ribbon and several strands of wool can be woven through some of the larger gaps. Wool and thread can be woven through some of the smaller spaces.
- The children will need to tie material at one end and weave through some of the gaps – it does not have to be regular. When finished, tie the material at the end so it does not come undone.

Andre Derain

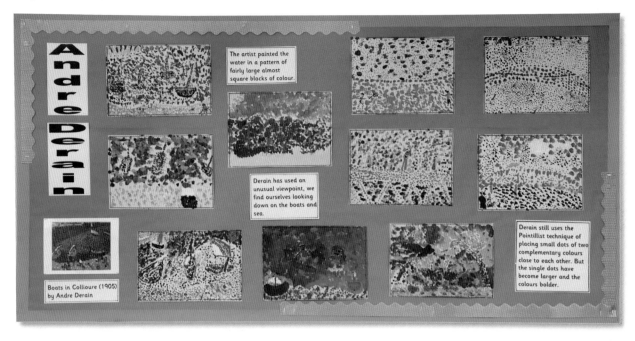

- Look at the painting *The Boat at Collioure* (1905) by French artist Andre Derain (1880–1954). Derain uses the pointillist technique (see page 65) of placing a quantity of small dots of two complementary colours close to each other. These blend together when viewed from a distance. Derain's single dots are rather large, almost square blocks of colour, and the colours are bright and bold. Derain used an unusual viewpoint – looking down on the boats and the sea.
- Compare the styles of painting of Georges Seurat (1859–91) and Andre Derain – they both use pointillism but the size of their dots varies.
- Look at how Derain has shown the pattern of the water by dabbing fairly large almost square blocks of colour close to each other. This technique is similar to how a mosaic builds up a picture using tiny pieces.
- Provide A3 sheets of white or yellow sugar paper. It is useful if the children can work in pairs to encourage ideas and conversation.
- Provide a variety of shades of blue paint and invite the children to choose any other colours they may need in their palette, adding a few drops at a time.
- Provide a variety of different-sized paintbrushes so the children can select the thickness of brush they want to use.

Water Collages

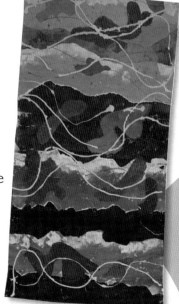

- Provide sugar paper, embossed wallpaper, paint in shades of blue and PVA glue mixed with blue or green food colouring.
- Invite the children to paint the papers in different shades of blue from light to dark.
- Next ask the children to rip a half-size piece of paper into five or six strips and paint these with the same colours, sticking them on their paper from dark to light.
- Cut out about six random watery shapes from white A4 paper for the children to use as a stencil. Ask them to put the stencil on the picture and sponge over it with any shades of blue. The printing will make a pattern or collage.
- Finally the children can drip coloured PVA glue onto the collage in wavy lines.

Seaside

A seaside theme lends itself well to geography and history links. Look at maps of the UK or the world and encourage the children to think about places they have visited. The seaside provides a great environment to compare with where the children live. Spend time looking for similarities and differences. Have seasides changed? What were they like in the past? What did people wear to the beach? Complete a timeline of what people have worn to the beach from 1900 to 2000.

Pirate Boy

- Read *Pirate Boy* by John Wallace (Harper Collins, 2002). This is a story about a young boy and his parrot who escape from two mean pirates that have captured them.
- Invite the children to create a display by making the items listed below.
- **Sea:** tear up shades of blue and green tissue paper and stick the strips onto A3 pieces of blue or green sugar paper. Completely cover the sugar paper, with layers of colour and overlap to achieve many different shades. Then cover with watered-down PVA glue – this will dry hard and give a shiny finish.
- **Sand:** sponge print paper with shades of yellow. Stick on some shells. Drip over with glue and add some gold glitter.
- **Palm tree:** paint a large tube with shades of brown. Stick large leaf shapes of green tissue paper on green palm-shaped sugar paper.

- **Boat:** paint strips of artificial wood flooring with green and blue paint. Alternatively, cut long strips of brown sugar paper then paint.
- Ask the children to cut out circles of card and bubble print with blue paint mixed with washing up liquid by blowing into the liquid and then printing onto the circles.
- Invite one group of children to paint seagulls that can be arranged on the picture and hung in front of the picture with some of the bubbles. Another group could paint crabs and other beach creatures.
- Add seaweed, coconuts and a cactus.
- Display the fish made from clay in the sea around the boat (see page 63).

3D Clay Fish

- Give each child a piece of clay to roll out with a rolling pin until approximately 1 cm thick.
- Pre-cut a few different shapes of fish on card for the children to cut around with a knife. Encourage the children to use these carefully, cutting right down to the board. They can then use a slice to push under the clay and lift the fish up. Any spare pieces of clay should be put to the side to use later for eyes, etc.
- Provide a range of printing tools for the children to put markings on the fish's body – kitchen tools, such as a potato masher, straining spoon and a slice, when pressed onto the clay makes interesting shapes. When the children have finished their markings, they can put a paper clip into the top to be able to hang the fish.

- Allow the fish to dry and when hard, ask the children to paint it with bright coloured paints.
- When dry, they can cover it with watered down PVA glue and sprinkle with glitter.

Shell Sculpture

- Collect the rectangular plastic lids from washing liquid tablet containers (or similar) and ask the children to bring in some shells.
- Mix a jug of plaster of Paris – do this away from the children as the dust rises when mixing with water. Pour clean luke warm water into a plastic container and gradually add the same quantity of plaster to the water until all the water has been absorbed.
- Pour the plaster of Paris into the lid containers and ask the children to carefully arrange the shells in the plaster. It will dry fast so the children need to place their shells quickly.

- When dry, the children can use green or blue food colouring to paint over the surface. Alternatively, the shells can be left and look very natural. Ask the children which option they prefer.
- Arrange the children's work in front of the display about *Pirate Boy*.

Swimming Turtles

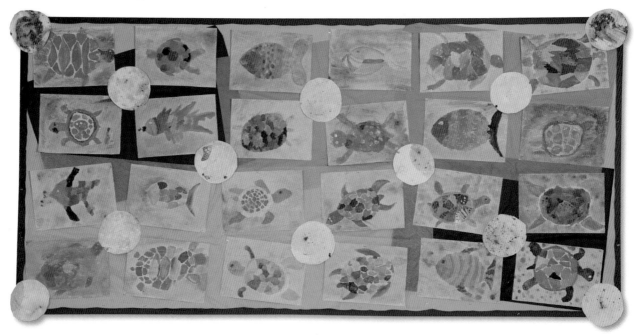

- Using a sheet of A3 watercolour paper, ask the children to draw an outline of a turtle's shell with markings, add a head, flippers and a tail with a blue pencil.
- They should paint the turtle with different shades of blue watercolour paint, adding dots of different colour so the paint will run.
- The paper around the turtle should be painted with plenty of clean water. While it is still wet, patches of green and turquoise paint can be added.
- The children can then either sprinkle salt over the wet paint or lay a layer of plastic foodwrap over the painting and leave to dry.
- When the paintings are completely dry, the children can pour off the salt or pull off the plastic foodwrap – this leaves an interesting crackled pattern over the sea.

Cross-curricular Links

- **Literacy** – Read the *Pirate Boy* story up to "Pirate Boy just scowled", then ask the children to write letters to the pirates asking them not to be so cruel to the Pirate Boy and suggesting kind things they could do for him.
- **PSHCE** – During circle time after reading the story, talk about how the two pirates have captured the boy and are making him do all the work on board the ship. Give

them time to talk about how the boy may feel and then write some questions on the whiteboard to ask the Pirate Boy. The teacher or a child could go into role as the boy and the other children could ask the questions.
- **Drama** – Ask the children to imagine playing on the beach before they are captured by some pirates. They will need to work out a clever plan of how to escape and what traps to set. This is a good opportunity to teach non-fiction writing, such as, how to write instructions. Ask the children to write a list of instructions for: What do we need? What should we do? What traps could we set?
- **Design & Technology** – Read up to "Time to set the traps!" and arrange the children into groups to talk about what traps they might invent to catch the pirates. Give them some paper to draw their designs and a range of materials to make their ideas.

Seurat

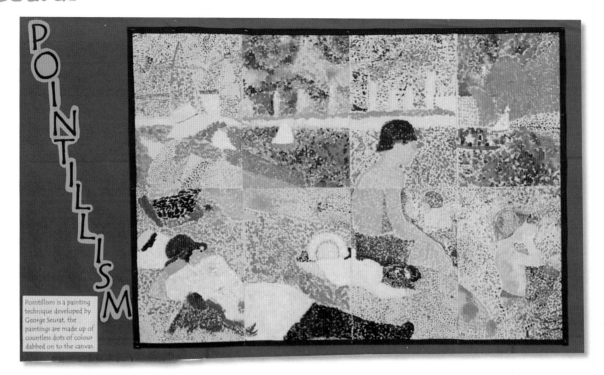

Pointillism is a painting technique developed by George Seurat; the paintings are made up of countless dots of colour dabbed on to the canvas.

- Georges Seurat (1859–91) developed the painting technique pointillism, which is similar to the image composed of many thousand of pixels on a television screen. The paintings are made up of dots of colour, dabbed laboriously on to the canvas. From a distance these dots blend together to form the picture and give the impression of different colours as they merge.
- Look at Seurat's paintings *Bathers at Asnières* (1883) and *La Grande Jatte* (1884). Discuss with the children the solid areas of colour and relatively simple shapes.
- Divide the painting *Bathers at Asnières* into eight equal pieces and draw the painting very simply on eight A2 pieces of sugar paper.
- Divide the children into groups of three or four to work on one section of the painting and encourage them to dab using the tip of a thin paint brush or the hard end if they prefer. By dabbing dots close together they will gain a stronger colour, while spacing the dots further apart will give a lighter colour when they step back from the painting.

- Encourage the children to mix the different colours they may need.
- Reassemble the sections with a frame and display on a large wall.
- Invite the children to choose an image from *Bathers at Asnières*, such as the boy sitting on the waters edge, to copy in pencil on A5 white paper.

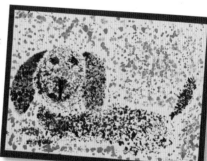

- Explain that they will need to use lots of close dots to get a darker image and space out the dots for a lighter image.
- Encourage them to just concentrate on the image to create the different shades of colour and not to worry about the background.

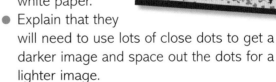

Cross-curricular Links

- **Literacy/ICT** – Ask the children to write a bibliography about Seurat. Use the Internet to access information about his short life and the unusual painting style he developed.

Journeys

This is a great theme when children begin a new academic year and have had a variety of experiences from the summer holidays. Invite the children to share their journey experiences, describing how they travelled and the countries they visited. A well-known book entitled *The Jolly Postman* by Janet and Allan Ahlberg (Puffin, 2002) is about a postman delivering his letters to a variety of interesting characters and provides an excellent starting point for this theme.

The Jolly Postman

Read the story to the children, stopping after each delivery to read the post that the postman delivered. Talk about the characters and decide which part of the story the children would like to make for a display. Discuss the order that the postman delivered the letters.

Below are a variety of ideas that can be used on the display:

Background
- On long sheets of green paper print with sponges in a variety of green shades.
- Print on shades of blue issue paper with white, silver and blue paint.
- Paint a road with brown paint mixed with sand and then print darker shades of brown on top to give a stone effect.

Landmarks
- Three Bears Cottage
- Gingerbread Bungalow

- Mile High House
- The Palace
- Grandma's Cottage
- Goldilocks House.

Detail
- Woods: collect branches to stick green leaves on from tissue, crepe and cellophane.
- Bears: cut a length of crepe paper of about 10cms. Create a fringe by making vertical cuts at regular intervals along the bottom edge of the long side which stop before the top edge. Stick the top edge down and the loose bits at the bottom will give the bears a furry 3D quality.
- Flowers: cut out a circle in sugar paper and stick petals around the edge in tissue and crepe paper. Decorate inside with rolled up pieces of tissue and lentils.

Maps

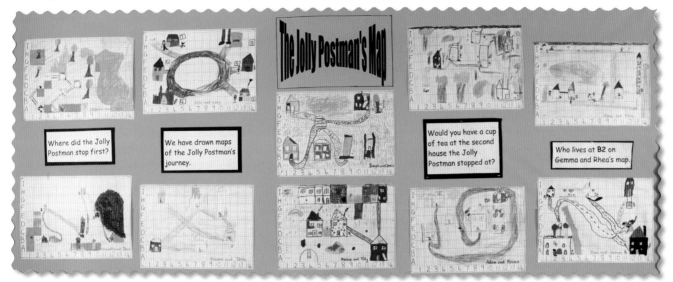

- In pairs, ask the children to create a map on squared A3 paper of the Jolly Postman's journey while delivering letters.
- They need to add co-ordinates along the top and bottom of the map, so they can locate the places on their maps.
- They can use felt-tip pens to draw the six homes that the postman visits.
- The road and detail can be added after the postman's journey is clearly marked.
- When the maps are complete, the children need to write the instruction for the Postman to move around their map. For example, start at A2, ^2 (up 2), >4 (right 4).

Cross-curricular Links

- **ICT** – A larger map can be made for the computer robot *Beebot*, to travel between the homes the postman delivers to.
  - Work on plans of the classroom with co-ordinates along the sides. Ask the children where, for example, the computer can be found. They will have to look at the co-ordinates along the top and bottom. Use co-ordinates to locate places on a grid or map. A 'pixie robot' would support this work well. Program the robot to move around shapes and around the classroom.

- **Geography** – Ask the children to draw their journey from home to school – this could be set as homework.
  - When looking at plans of the school, ask the children to find the shortest route between two classrooms.

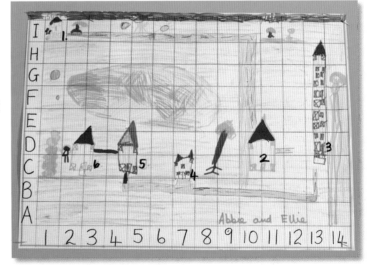

  - Encourage the children to recognise some of the physical and human features in their locality – these can be compared to the story.
- **Literacy** – Ask the children to learn their address and compare these to the addresses the postman delivers letters to in the story.
  - Investigate different street and town names, as well as postcodes. What do they mean?

Trees

Trees are a fascinating changing theme for children to study. They are as individual as people. If you were describing a friend, you would talk about their hair, eyes, height, etc. To describe a tree you need similar detail – the leaves, flowers, twigs, shape of trunk and texture of the bark. The growth patterns vary with different trees – Which way do the branches point? Where are the longest branches? How thick are the branches? Trees come in many different shapes. Begin observing trees in winter when the branches are bare. Follow the changing cycle of the trees – watch out for new buds and blossom in spring, leading on to comparing the shapes of the leaves and trees in the middle of summer. Finally, in the autumn, the leaves change colour and fall off the trees, ready to begin the cycle again.

Season Tree: Winter

This display helps the children learn the different seasons displayed in a quarter of the tree. This activity will take a few days to cover each season and can be linked to class maths work on time and seasons.

- Using A5 pieces of grey card, ask the children to place a little spoonful of runny black paint at the bottom of the page in the middle – this will be the trunk of the tree. Next they should use a plastic straw to blow the paint up the paper. The blob will travel in a line but then split and shoot off to form branches. By changing the angle of their blowing, they will create various branches spreading from the trunk.
- Collect four large branches from a horse chestnut tree and put them in a bucket on

the floor for the children to decorate. Pre-cut white tissue circles with a diameter of about 10 cm for the children to cut out as snowflakes. Demonstrate making a snowflake by folding each circle in half, then a quarter, and then an eighth and cutting little holes along the two edges. Open up the circle and the snowflake has a doily effect. Hang the snowflakes on the branches.

Season Tree: Spring

- Pick four large branches and put in a pot on the floor so the children can decorate them easily. This time, cut out various shades of pink tissue paper in 10 cm circles with a curly edge. Ask the children to fold and cut them, as with the snowflake, and these can hang on the tree as blossom. Cut out a few lime green leaves for the children to stick onto the branches as the new growth on spring trees.

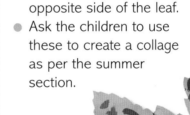

- Ask the children to cut out the six egg holders from a cardboard egg box and paint them yellow. They should attach these with a split pin to a piece of yellow crepe paper that has been cut out with four or five petals like a daffodil. Invite the children to stick these on a stem with long leaves cut out of sugar paper.

Season Tree: Summer

- Pre-cut green sugar paper leaves and drop them in some green marbling ink. The ink will give the leaves a shiny texture.
- Ask the children to create a collage using the green sugar paper leaves with green tissue, crepe, shiny and cellophane paper. Cover the sugar paper so the summer leaves have a rich, full texture.

- Make a few flowers to go along the edge of the summer leaves. Cut out circles on card and decorate around the edge with petals of crepe paper. Use rice, lentils or seeds to decorate the middle of the flower.

Season Tree: Autumn

- On A5 size black paper, ask the children to paint a glowing autumn picture of a tree with leaves in all sorts of shades of orange, yellow, red and brown. They should paint a knobbly tree trunk with branches in brown and then dab on overlapping splodges of autumn colours for the leaves with the end of the paint brush.
- Pre-cut leaf shaped pieces of white paper and marble with marbling inks using red, yellow and orange ink.
- Pre-cut leaf-shaped pieces of orange sugar paper and ask the children to paint on one side of the leaf with red, yellow and orange paint and then fold the leaf in half – the pattern will print on the opposite side of the leaf.
- Ask the children to use these to create a collage as per the summer section.

Charles Burchfield

Charles Burchfield (1893–1967) was an American painter known particularly for his watercolours, which show intense, boldly drawn portrayals of nature using just a few colours. Weather and sunlight effects are important in all his work and the

paintings have a mystical feel.

- Look at Burchfield's paintings *Orion in December* (1959) and *Sultry Moon* (1959). Although he used only a few colours, the artist managed to catch the wintry feeling. Earth and sky seem to meet in Burchfield's pictures. The stars have slipped down among the trees and are reflected by twinkling snowflakes on the ground.
- Provide each child with an A5 piece of blue sugar paper, a palette with black, white, blue and yellow paint, an extra palette to mix various shades of the different colours, paint brushes of different thicknesses for the detail and a pot of water.
- Encourage the children to start with a tree shape and to think about the many different shapes observed during a walk around the school. They should paint the tree in dark shades and use the other colours to add light and shadows to the picture. Discuss

where the light is coming from – the stars or the moon? Ask the children how it would fall on the branches and the ground – which side of the tree would it light up? Gradually the shapes and colours will make a wintery mystical painting.

Silhouettes

- Ask the children to paint stripes of cold winter colours such as blues, purples and greys on an A3 piece of paper. They can then create the outline of a winter tree in collage using black sugar paper, black tissue and crepe paper.
- Provide different shades of grey sugar paper cut to A5 size. Ask the children to cut out a white moon and place it on the picture. Then create the outline of a tree. They should concentrate on giving an interesting shape to the tree. Detail such as a fence, land formations and simple animals can then be added.

Wire Sculptures

- Provide some modelling wire cut into 25 cm strips.
- Give each child at least ten strips. Invite the children to hold one strip and wind another around the wire leaving a length at the top to arrange as branches. They should keep adding the wires by wrapping around the initial wire to gradually become thicker and make a trunk. The lengths at the top can be left free so the children can arrange them later when they can see the finished trunk and have decided on the shape of the branches.
- After wrapping all the wires together, the children should place the end into a piece of plasticine so the tree will stand up. This makes it easier to arrange the branches in interesting shapes. The children can then work with each separate piece of wire bending it into the shape they want.

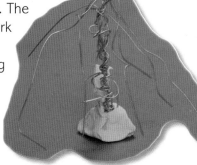

Large Plastic Bag Trees

- As part of a Design and Technology topic, 'Trees' is a great theme to stimulate the children's ideas and organisation skills. Begin by explaining what resources will be available to them and discuss the tools they may use, emphasising any safety issues, e.g. How do we use the tools safely?
- Invite them to create individual designs, focusing on how the trees would be put together and what tools they may use. Consider the possibility of measuring and how they will attach the various materials with the tools provided.
- Divide the children into groups and show each group what resources they will have and ask them to create their own group design, incorporating any ideas they may have had previously. Encourage them to consider in what order they may do things and then write the instructions as a group.
  - Group 1: wire trees. Provide buttons and bottle tops, chicken wire, strong plastic garden wire, plastic tape, thin wire, hammer and nails and pliers.
  - Group 2: plastic and cane shrubs. Provide plaster of Paris, garden canes, green plastic bags, wire and a bucket.
  - Group 3: paper and plastic trees. Provide cardboard tubes, plastic bags, a large umbrella, large metal tins, masking tape/sellotape, glue, garden wire, newspaper, paint and varnish.
- When finished, encourage the children to evaluate their trees. How does it compare to the design? What are the good points? What would they improve? Invite the children to test the sturdiness of the trees.

71

Winter Wonderland Picture

- Begin the lesson by taking the children outside and standing under a big thick tree. Encourage them to look up and describe how the branches come out of the trunk. Ask them to use their hands to show the upward movement and growth of the branches. Point out how some of the branches of the tree come down towards the ground, bending and branching at many points, while the branches of other trees fan out and then travel upwards.
- Demonstrate several ways that young children draw trees, such as a lollypop tree. Discuss the branches being a part of the tree and how they are not just stuck on – tempting as it may be to draw them like that. Talk about the different shapes of trees from a beech to a poplar.
- Give each child a piece of tracing paper about 10 cm square and a pencil.
- Ask them to make a pencil drawing of a tree in winter on the tracing paper. They should begin with a small trunk and add branches that gradually spread out.
- When the children have added enough detail, cut around the tree and arrange the children's trees on a large piece of tracing paper that can then be framed. The trees can be arranged in front of and overlapping each other to build up the impression of a wood.
- These look very effective displayed on a window so the light shines through.

Cross-curricular Links

- **Science** – Look at the life cycle of a tree. Encourage the children to follow the changes throughout the year. Ask them to draw the cycle of the tree by showing the leaves, flowers and seeds at different times.